MAYFLOWER REMEMBERED

A History of the Plymouth Pilgrims

MAYFLOWER REMEMBERED

A History of the Plymouth Pilgrims

by

CRISPIN GILL

DAVID & CHARLES : NEWTON ABBOT

7153 4726 8

285.91

Set in ten on twelve point Pilgrim
and printed in Great Britain
by Clarke, Doble & Brendon Limited Plymouth
for David & Charles (Publishers) Limited
South Devon House Newton Abbot Devon

For Gladys and Charles
who made it possible

NOTE: Where sums of money in English or American currencies appear the equivalent in the other currency is given in parenthesis at the 1970 rate of exchange. The comparison of values between 1620 and 1970 is not simple, but probably present-day prices are between eight and twelve times 1620 values. Multiplying the old figures by ten will give a rough and ready understanding.

Contents

List of Illustrations

PLATES

List of Illustrations

TEXT FIGURES

MAPS AND PLANS

List of Illustrations

Introduction

PILGRIMS have an old and honourable link with the name of Plymouth. English men and women took passage in the town's wine ships bound for Bordeaux to ride on down across the Landes and over the Pyrenees to the tomb of St James of Compostello, in north-western Spain. Their badge was the scallop-shell, in shape not unlike the clams which in a later century were to sustain other Pilgrims on the shores of New England. In turn the ships brought back European pilgrims, bound for the tomb of St Thomas à Becket at Canterbury. The parish church of Plympton St Maurice, five miles from Plymouth on the London road, was originally dedicated to St Thomas à Becket, as still is the church of Kingswear, across the river from Dartmouth. But Plymouth was the important town for the outgoing pilgrims, and in 1389 it was named with Dover as the only two ports by which people could leave the country.

Though this business lasted a century or more, and the Pilgrims to New England were only in the port a few days, it is they who have left their mark on Plymouth. As a native I have used the name 'Mayflower' since earliest childhood. I caught my first fish (with a rod and line bought for a few pence in Charlie Cload's low-ceilinged, cluttered-up ship-chandler's shop on the fish quay), sitting with my little legs dangling over the end of the Mayflower Pier. Before I was ten I was sculling the dinghy men of the Mayflower Sailing Club out to their boats. In my late 'teens when I shared a tubby little cruiser we would moor it in front of the Mayflower and walk across to its little bar for our evening pint. Today I buy my books in Mayflower Street. The name crops up a dozen times in the Plymouth telephone directory, covering antique shops, hairdressers, garages, plasterers, sandwich bars, even engineers. Only 'Drake' has been more used as an emotive name.

Yet Plymouth had been playing its part in North American history for half a century and more before *Mayflower* made her chance call at the English port. Her own sons and neighbours had played as important a part in opening up the New World as these strangers. The first Englishmen to trade across the Atlantic were the Hawkins family of Plymouth, yet they have no memorial in the city, not even a tavern named after them. In the United States one finds a similar state of affairs; the men and women of the *Mayflower* are the Founding Fathers, yet Virginia had been settled for fourteen years when they arrived, and within ten years a bigger settlement around Massachusetts Bay was completely to eclipse them.

It was to clarify this riddle that I set out upon this book. Where did they come from, why did they go, how did they go, what did they do, what happened to them? These were questions that had to be answered before the riddle could even be understood.

Page 17 (*above*) All that remains of the manor house at Scrooby, the home of William Brewster; (*below right*) the inn sign and church steeple at Scrooby; (*left*) the street leading to Boston Guildhall where the Pilgrims were imprisoned

Page 18 Holland : (*above*) the Leyden garden round which the Pilgrims lived, with the roof of St. Peter's Church visible over the top of the Jean Pesijn Hof; (*below*) the Voorhaven at Delftshaven, whence the *Speedwell* sailed

CHAPTER ONE

The True Church

THE REFORMATION of the church in England came when
ordinary men and women could read, or have read to them,
the Bible in their own language. Then they could think for
themselves, test the teachings of the church, and move away from
the incomprehensible Latin of the church service. It had nothing
to do with the formal break with Rome made by King Henry VIII
in 1535; that was merely the way in which he could legalise his
marriage to one wife and his marrying the next. Henry remained
a Catholic all his life, as in reality did his two children who came
of age, Mary and Elizabeth. Mary took the church and the country
back into the arms of Rome when she was on the throne; Henry
and Elizabeth were sturdy enough and English enough to resent any
foreign domination of any part of their realm but they still said,
as does every Anglican and Episcopalian worshipper today, 'I believe in . . . the holy Catholick Church'.

They were realists enough to know that if they threw off the
yoke of religious authority, as represented by the Pope, they were
showing the way to their own subjects to throw off their authority.
The Church of England made the monarch its head; for the State
did not mind people having their own ideas in religion so long as
its own authority was not challenged. The danger was that doubts
about things spiritual could lead to doubts about things temporal,
and that the State, which in those times also meant the Crown,
could not tolerate.

The struggle went back long before Henry VIII. Wyclif in the
fourteenth century was attacking the church, and Chaucer in his
Canterbury Tales was laughing at the churchmen among his pilgrims when the travellers to Santiago de Compostello had been
sailing out of Plymouth. Wyclif preached that the Bible was the
only source of religious truth and his followers produced the first

Bible in the English language but like the subsequent translations it remained an illegal book, banned by the Crown—men who thought about the church could also think about the State.

One great result of Henry's break with Rome was that he had to demonstrate his acceptance of the reformed church by permitting first an English Bible, and then an English Prayer Book. Throughout the reforming zeal of the men who ruled England for the boy-king Edward VI, the fires of Smithfield kindled by Mary Tudor's return to Rome, and the middle-of-the-road policy of the Elizabethan church settlement, one can see the Bible fermenting in the minds of men. Not only the gentlemen and the priests could read; the new grammar schools brought a further spreading of literacy. All could listen and by law had to attend church even if the parson did not preach on the Bible (or even did not preach at all), the new Prayer Books laid down long portions of the Scriptures to be read at every service. Echoes of the Bible can be heard in every letter and recorded speech of the time. Many of the Protestants who had gone underground in Mary's reign became the people who would not accept Elizabeth's church; it is significant that thirteen years after her accession such people could still be found—but in the prisons of London.

Elizabeth would have gone back to the church of her father but England had moved too far for this. Her first Parliament insisted on the second Prayer Book of Edward VI; the Queen made sure that it was sufficiently modified to be acceptable to the High Church party. Catholic pressures at home and abroad forced her to move to the left in church matters but she had little time for the growing Puritan party in the country. The Catholics who were executed died because they were foreign agents, traitors, threats to the safety of England, rather than for their religion. But under these threats from Catholic countries to the security of England, and with the Bible available in the English language for forty years past, the mass of the people were moving away from the Catholic ideas. All truth, they believed, was to be found in the Scriptures; a man could talk direct to God without need of a priest as intercessor, and they saw as idolatory such things as vestments, the sign of the cross, the giving of a ring in marriage, or kneeling at communion.

So Elizabeth's church began to enforce a sharp discipline on priests and people to conform. The Queen especially felt that any disagreement with the principles of the church was an attack on her as its head. Those who believed that religion was an individual faith began to deny the supremacy of the State in such matters and under the leadership of Robert Browne began to withdraw from the church. They were called Separatists, Congregations of Independents, or Brownists after their leader. Browne eventually went back to the church but his movement grew. Several of his followers were executed in 1593, and an Act of Parliament that year made attendance at such conventicles punishable with banishment. Some, to escape the persecution that became their life, escaped into Holland where there was freedom for men to worship as they pleased. Others struggled on.

When James VI of Scotland became King of England on Elizabeth's death in 1603, both the Catholics and the Protestant party of the Church of England had high hopes. The Protestants, declaring that they were no Puritans or Brownists, made massive demands on him. In their self-righteousness they did not reckon with the new man's temper; he had striven with the Presbyterians in Scotland for years and believed not only in the divine right of kings but the divine right of bishops too. So the Protestants got no change. The Catholics found no help in him either and their exasperation led to the Gunpowder Plot of 1605, when the conspirators hoped to blow up both the stiff-necked king and his protestant House of Commons. The Separatists found themselves more oppressed than ever.

These dissenters were not confined to the universities, or to the big cities. Even in the remote rural areas of Lincolnshire and Yorkshire, where in 1536 the simple people had risen in what is remembered as the Pilgrimage of Grace against any departure from their old familiar church services, the new ideas were spreading. It is in the fertile Midland plains where Lincolnshire and Yorkshire and Nottinghamshire meet that the story of the Mayflower Pilgrims begins.

GAINSBOROUGH AND SCROOBY

Although far inland, Gainsborough is a river port on the wide river Trent, which flows north to the Humber estuary. Around its church

Tudor gravestones still describe the dead as 'mariner, of this port'. Through all the ports of England the advanced Calvinistic ideas of Europe and particularly the Low Countries flowed in. A Puritan family lived in Old Hall, still standing just across from the church, and in the town the Rev John Smyth became the leader of a Sepa-

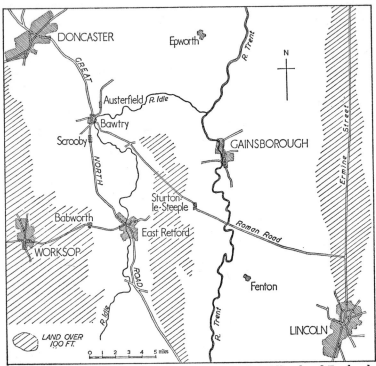

Sketch-map of the Scrooby area in the north Midlands of England, where the Pilgrims originated

ratist congregation possibly as early as 1602. He was a Cambridge man and a notable preacher; after ten years in a Yorkshire parish he was appointed lecturer at Lincoln in 1600 but was deprived of office after two years.

In the area there were also beneficed clergy of similar views, notably the Rev Richard Bernard of Worksop who wrote an allegory in the vein which Bunyan was to follow with his *Pilgrim's Progress*, and the Rev Richard Clifton who was in trouble at Babworth for refusing to observe fully the ceremonies of the church. There were other clergy on both sides of Trent becoming alienated from the church, but many like Bernard were to draw back from the final step of separation. There were also laymen whose conscience was taking them from the church, and chief among them was William Brewster, the postmaster of Scrooby.

Scrooby is a forgotten village now, with redbrick houses scattered higgledy-piggledy about the parish church with its dumpy stone steeple. Herds of cows are driven home at milking time along its meandering, one-car-wide main street. It was by-passed first by the eighteenth-century turnpike which runs on the other side of the church, then by the main line of the Great Northern Railway, along which the Edinburgh expresses still thunder a few yards from the old Brewster back door. In recent years the Doncaster by-pass which speeds the cars and trucks along a six-lane motorway has further isolated it. But before these changes this narrow street was the Great North Road from London to York and Edinburgh, and this gave the village its importance. Even its river, the Idle, was navigable for small craft and provided local links through Bawtry, the river port a mile or so away, north-east to the main stream of the Trent, and southwards to Retford. The canal age later replaced the Idle just as the turnpikes killed the old North Road. Bawtry lost its port but seized the coaching trade; Scrooby was left with nothing. The Archbishop of York owned much of the land in the neighbourhood and in the village he had a manor house, a minor palace which was his residence in the southern part of his province. Margaret Tudor, Henry VIII's sister, stayed in this timber house on her way north to marry James IV of Scotland, Cardinal Wolsey spent a month there shortly before his downfall, and King Henry himself had been a guest.

After this brief spell of glory the house had been leased by Archbishop Sandys to his son, and John Brewster, postmaster of Scrooby, was appointed receiver and bailiff of the estate. As postmaster, his duty was to maintain relays of horses with which to speed the Queen's messengers riding north and south along the road. The Pony Express of frontier America has ancient origins! From carrying the royal mail the post was beginning to handle private correspondence; private travellers were glad to hire horses, and the manor house served as an inn affording food and rest along the road.

John Brewster sent his son William, who was born in 1566 or 1567, to Cambridge, but he left at an early age and entered the service of Sir William Davison, one of Queen Elizabeth's ministers. How he reached such early preferment is unknown, but it is quite possible that Davison, travelling the Great North Road in 1583, had seen the young man and divined his ability. Certainly on a mission to the Netherlands in 1585 Davison had young Brewster in close attendance, and the young man remained there when Davison returned in 1586 to become assistant to Walsingham, the queen's Secretary of State, and as such in daily attendance on the queen. For William Brewster the future was bright; his master 'imployed him in all matters of greatest trust and secrecie. He esteemed him rather as a sonne than a servante. . . .' But the queen made Davison a scapegoat for the execution of Mary Queen of Scots; in 1587 he was in the Tower and Brewster was back with his father in Scrooby.

In 1590 William succeeded his father as postmaster, though not before Davison had intervened on his behalf with the authorities. For eighteen years he was to hold this office on the Great North Road, small beer after life at court, riding in ambassadorial processions with a gold chain about his neck, sleeping with the keys of surrendered Dutch cities under his pillow, but they were not wasted years. He had been at Cambridge, that fermenting ground of Puritan ideas in the church. His patron Davison was a convinced Puritan and had links with the exiled Separatist church in Holland. Brewster, with his strong family background in Scrooby, his position of local authority, and his brief acquaintance with the great men of the day, would have been a figure of respect in the neighbourhood.

He did much good in ye countrie wher he lived, in promoting and furthering religion, not only by his practiss & example, and provocking and incouraging of others, but by procuring of good preachers to ye places thereabout, and drawing on of others to assiste & help forward in such a worke; he him selfe most comonly deepest in yet charge. . .

This quotation, and our knowledge of Brewster when in Davison's employ, comes from the obituary written by John Bradford on Brewster's death. Bradford was born in Austerfield, a scattered village a mile or two north of Bawtry. Within a year of his birth in 1590, the year that 23 year-old Brewster became postmaster, Bradford was orphaned. Among his eventual four guardians was a neighbour of Brewster's at Scrooby, and in the fullness of time the boy Bradford was an associate of Brewster there.

The last figure to appear on the scene is John Robinson. Born at Sturton-le-Steeple, a lonely village on the left bank of the Trent a few miles upstream from Gainsborough, he was of good yeoman stock like both Brewster and Bradford. He too was educated at Cambridge, staying on after graduating as a Fellow of Corpus Christi. During his twelve years in the university the great debate on the church was in full cry, and in this the young dean played his part. No doubt he hoped, like the great Protestant divines preaching and lecturing in the university, to reform the church from within. The year in which King James came to the throne and declared he would have no truck with the Puritans, Robinson resigned his Fellowship and married Bridget White of Fenton, a village just across the Trent from his home. There were still Fentons at Fenton Hall and Captain Edward Fenton had commanded the *Mary Rose* in the Armada battles, married the sister-in-law of the great John Hawkins of Plymouth, Treasurer of the Navy, and had led the first expedition planned to exploit Drake's voyage round the world.

With his young bride Robinson moved to Norwich, another centre of Protestant belief. He was still feeling his way, and though he rejected the strong views of the Calvinists he equally could not accept the Arminian, High Church view that the king and his bishops were seeking to thrust upon the Anglicans. In a very short time Robinson was suspended for refusing to conform to the new Book of Canons of 1604. He went home. He was still an Anglican minister, much troubled in the mind.

Robinson was not alone in this, John Smyth was holding meetings at Gainsborough away from the church. Brewster and Richard Clifton had been attending them but it was a 9 mile journey each way for both of them so other meetings began to be held in

Brewster's house at Scrooby and Robinson began to join them. Even the six miles from Babworth to Scrooby was probably often too much for Clifton who was now an old man. For Robinson it meant a 9 mile walk up the old Roman road from Lincoln to Doncaster, which leads from his village to Scrooby over the low range of hills separating the Trent valley from its tributary the Idle, but he was a younger man. He was still undecided; he paid a visit to Cambridge and listening and talking to the leaders of Protestant thought there helped to resolve his mind. Somewhere about 1606 he, Smyth, and Clifton separated from the Church of England. It caused a considerable stir locally, and the pressure was on.

> For some were taken & clapt up in prison, others had their houses besett & watcht night and day, & hardly escaped their hands; and ye most were faine to flie and leave their howses & habitations, and the means of their livelehood . . . seeing themselves thus molested, and that ther was no hope of their continuance ther, by a joynte consente they resolved to goe into ye Low-Countries, wher they heard was freedome of Religion for all men : as also how sundrie from London & other parts of ye land, had been exiled and persecuted for ye same cause, & were gone thither, and lived at Amsterdam, & in other places of ye land.

Those who were caught appeared in the courts of the Archbishop of York and languished in his prison; it is ironic that one of the meeting houses was on his own property. Brewster lost his job as postmaster, and was fined £20 ($48) for being 'disobedient in matters of religion'; a daughter born to him and his wife at this time was christened Fear. Both the Scrooby and the Gainsborough congregations were resolved to seek their freedom in exile. The exodus was not easy. The ports were shut against them; so by stealth they had to contact seamen to take them, and pay bribes and extortionate rates on the way. Smyth and his friends made the journey first; they had the advantage of living in a port.

THE FLIGHT TO HOLLAND

Eventually in 1607 a ship was hired by the Scrooby people which would embark them near Boston, on the flat and empty shores of the Wash. The 60 mile journey must have been slow and arduous, past the triple-towered bulk of Lincoln Cathedral on its hilltop, across the rich farmlands of the Fens. They stole aboard the ship by night, but the master had betrayed them. They were seized, thrust into small boats, and subjected to cheap indignities by the officers, 'searching them to their shirts for money, yea even the women furder than became modestie.' They were hauled into Boston as a spectacle for the flocking mob, thrust before the magistrates, and messengers were sent to inform the Privy Council of their arrest. The magistrates were sympathetic, for there were strong Puritan leanings in Boston, and treated them as kindly as they could, but they had no choice but to keep them in the cells under the Guildhall until word came from London. So they waited a month; then all were released save seven, who were sent to the Assizes. Brewster, Robinson and Clifton were among them, but they were set free.

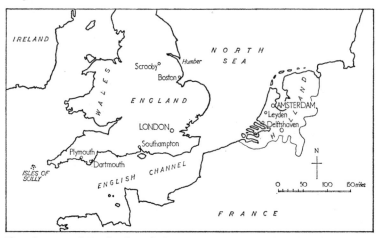

Sketch-map of England and the Low Countries, showing the towns which saw the Pilgrims, 1608-20

No doubt they made their way back to their own countryside until the next spring, when another attempt was made. In spite of the hardships they had undergone, others had joined them. Now agreement was made with a Dutch ship-owner at Hull, who agreed to pick them up on the lonely marshes on the south shore of the

Humber. This time the women and children, with the household goods, went down the Idle by boat, and the men walked. When the women arrived the ship was not at the rendezvous, so their boat took shelter in a small creek near Grimsby, only to stick on the mud when the tide went out. Next morning, when the ship did arrive, they were still aground and could not get afloat till midday. The master embarked the men, whom he had seen on the shore, but scarcely was the first boatload aboard when another large group of men, some armed, some on horseback, were seen bearing down on them. Without hesitation the Dutchmen weighed anchor and sailed. The few men embarked had nothing but the clothes in which they stood and scarce a penny in their pockets, for everything was in the boat with the women. To add to their fears for the wives and children they had left, a storm struck them and they were driven right across to the Norwegian coast. It was fourteen days before they made harbour in Holland.

Of their comrades left on shore some had scattered and escaped, some had gone to help the women. These were all arrested, weeping for their husbands so taken from them, to endure again the miseries of the mob and the prison. They were harried from place to place, from one magistrate to another, but no one knew what to do with them. They could not be sent home, for their homes had been sold up. Not only did it seem inhuman to keep them in prison, but public indignation was rising on their behalf. In the end the authorities were glad to see them go, and cross to Holland and their husbands. Yet their plight, and the second spell of imprisonment, brought them much sympathy, and attracted still more to the cause.

CHAPTER TWO

Exile in Holland

BREWSTER AND ROBINSON were the last to join their Scrooby flock in Amsterdam. They stayed back to see the little group off, by different ways and at different times, helping the weakest before they moved themselves. Even now the adventures were not over. Young Bradford found his way across to Holland without too much difficulty but once arrived found himself arrested again and accused of having fled out of England. On hearing his reasons, however, the magistrates discharged him and he got to Amsterdam. Few of the newcomers, simple country people, were happy in this large city, with its strange language and customs and no call for their rural skills. They saw 'the grime & grisly face of povertie coming upon them like an armed man'.

Nor were the English already there of overmuch comfort. Apart from the 'ancient church' which had arrived from England in 1597, there was another group from the borders of Wiltshire, Gloucestershire and Somerset, as well as John Smyth and the neighbours from Gainsborough. Not only moral scandals were shaking the 'ancient church' but fierce religious issues were splitting them all. When men claim the right to interpret the Bible for themselves each finds a different answer. In the fullness of time these Separatists from the Church of England were to split into Presbyterians, Baptists, Congregationalists and Unitarians; the second great break-away from the Church of England produced three or four kinds of Methodists before the re-union of this century, and any Saturday evening paper shows in its religious notices, even in the present ecumenical times, how widely rent is the left wing of the church.

Richard Clifton did his best to unite the quarrelling factions but Robinson and Brewster resolved that the only way to hold their flock together was to move from Amsterdam. Leyden, as a university city, attracted them. Their application to move there in February 1609 was granted by the city fathers provided that they 'behave themselves and submit to the laws and ordinances'. The move was made in April. Clifton stayed in Amsterdam; he was still at heart a member of their congregation but he was 'a grave and fatherly old man . . . having a great white beard . . . loath to remove any more'. He died in Amsterdam seven years later. Bradford wrote this pen-picture forty years later, and in the same *Discourse* recorded that John Smyth and his Gainsborough people, after first opposing the 'ancient church' in Amsterdam, joined first them and afterwards the Dutch Baptists. Smyth died in 1612 and his flock disintegrated.

Leyden, a miniature Amsterdam with almost as many canals as it has narrow cobbled streets, hump-backed bridges and crowded redbrick houses, enfolds the confluence of the Old and New Rhine around the embattled little hill between them. Moats shaped like a castle wall enclose the old city as a further defence, and only

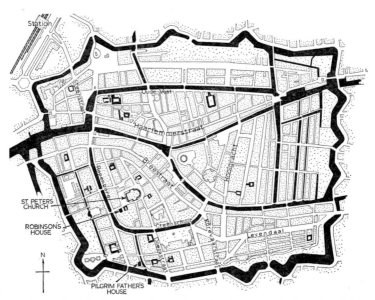

Leyden: the black areas show the Old Rhine and the New Rhine flowing in from the right to meet in the centre of the town, and the canals which were cut to make water defences round the town

thirty years before this little English group arrived the city had played a vital rôle in the Dutch fight against their Spanish oppressors.

The Leyden records show them settling quietly into the town. Within a few years more English recruits flocked to them, from London, Colchester, Suffolk and Kent. Marriages began to be celebrated, the vows being made in the Dutch way before a magistrate. Robinson, now the accepted pastor, held that marriage was not a sacrament of the church, and civic marriage before the magistrate was one of the customs later taken into the New World. The marriage records show the occupations they followed: blacksmith, fustian-worker, hatter, twiner, tailor, mason, weaver, baize-worker, glover. Some were the old trades of the new recruits from English towns, others are clearly ones which country people could adopt. Bradford apprenticed himself to a French silk-worker until he came of age, could realise his little estate in England and set up on his own account.

Robinson bought a house called Groene Port, in the Kloksteeg (the House with the Green Door, in Clock Lane) running from the cathedral-like Church of St Peter down to a bridge over a canal and the university. The house was big enough to serve as a dwelling-house for Robinson and his family, and as a church and meeting place for the community. In the big garden they built twenty-one tenements, so that many of the English families lived close together in this foreign city. Robinson stretched his mind in debate on religious principles with the Dutch reformers, writing pamphlets to confound some of the arguments put forward by the other English churches in Holland. While many moved to extreme views the Leyden community remained tolerant and liberal; they were willing to pray with people who did not share their views, and to go to any church if they could there hear a good preacher.

In many ways they were so little removed from the Anglican Church of the day that in 1614 there were hopes that, with the new Parliament, they might be able to return to England. But James dissolved that Parliament in a very short time, and thenceforward the Puritans and the English Crown moved further and further apart. Instead of going back the Leyden church was welcoming new members from England; from Chichester, Cambridge, Sandwich, London, Colchester and York. Among the newcomers of 1615 were Robert Cushman a Canterbury wool-comber, and Thomas Brewer, a landowner of some standing. Both Robinson and Brewer became members of Leyden University in that year, and within a couple of years Brewer bought the Groenehuis (The Green House) two doors away from Robinson.

Brewer financed the setting up of a press which Brewster operated from 1616 onwards. A master printer called Reynolds was brought over from London and with him came 22 year-old Edward Winslow as an assistant. Winslow's family were landowners and farmers near Droitwich, and he was educated at the King's School, Worcester. In 1613 he was apprenticed to a London printer but must have broken his indentures to go to Holland. The Amsterdam Separatists had long operated a printing press. The Leyden press was set up at 15 Pieterskerkkoorsteeg (Peter's Church Choir Street) between St Peter's Church and the Town Hall, and the premises were linked with Brewster's house in the Stinksteeg. Only three publications bore the printer's name and address. The rest, printed in English, bore no imprint for they contained the religious ideas Brewster knew only too well would not be approved by the English authorities.

PLANNING TO MOVE

By 1617 the people behind the Green Door were beginning to doubt their future in Leyden. Life was not easy there; some of the new recruits went home again and age began to take its toll of the original community. The children were growing up exposed to the temptations of the city, and were not willing to accept the burdens that their parents bore. It was clear that even if the children grew up as good Protestants, they would eventually be Dutch Protestants, and not English. The religious disputes among the Dutch at times threatened civil war, and the truce with Spain was coming to an end.

Across the Atlantic the English colony at Jamestown was beginning to flourish. There was much propaganda circulating concerning north Virginia, which had just been renamed New England, as yet unsettled but offering a climate more suitable for Englishmen to work in than that further south. Then there was the fabled land of Guiana; Sir Walter Ralegh had sailed off that very spring, in a last search for his El Dorado. If, the Leyden people debated among themselves, they removed their congregation to the New World they would be free to worship as they wished, free from the dangers of their present situation, and able to take the Gospel to the heathen Indians. Against this, other members argued the lack of capital to finance the move, the length of the journey, the perils of the sea, and the savagery of the Indians. Would this be greater even than the cruelty of Catholic Spanish soldiery in a new war? The emigration argument won; but where to go? Guiana was very hot, and the Spanish would not tolerate settlers there. Virginia was more suitable, but how free would they be there from the king's interference? In the autumn of 1617, while Ralegh was still struggling in the marshes of the Orinoco, the Leyden people sent two deacons to London to sound out the authorities. They were John Carver, originally a merchant from Doncaster, eight miles north of Scrooby, first mentioned in Leyden documents in 1616, a man of 'singular piety and rare for humilitie', and Robert Cushman.

Their first need was to convince people that they were a reasonable and not extreme body, so the two envoys took with them 'seven articles' in which Robinson and Brewster set out the religious principles of the community. In this they accepted the confession of the faith of the Church of England and all its articles; and that this faith could save both conformists and reformists, with all of whom they desired to stay in communion and peace. They accepted the king's authority and that no one could decline or appeal from it, his right to appoint bishops and civil authorities.

The authority of the present Bishops in the land we do acknowledge so far forth as the same is indeed derived from His Majesty unto them, and as they proceed in his name whom we will also therein honour in all things and him in them.

They believed that no synod or convocation had any authority save what was given them by the magistrates, and they desired to give unto all superiors due honour 'to preserve the unity of the spirit with all that fear God'.

It is hard reading this to see what had taken them out of the Church of England. It appears the statement of honest men, given without equivocation. London asked about their methods of government, and were told that they claimed pastors for teaching, elders for ruling, deacons for distributing the churches' contributions, and the two sacraments of baptism and the Lord's supper. The ministers prayed with their heads uncovered, their elders were chosen from men who could teach, although they were not required to do so, and like the deacons were chosen in perpetuity. The elders administered their office in admonitions and excommunication for scandals, publicly and before the congregation. Baptism was only given to a child of whom one parent at least was a member of some church.

The Privy Councillors who gave ear to the men from Leyden began to be mollified, and the general understanding was that the king would not give them his public authority, but he would connive at their going and not molest them. However, the Virginia Company had its own problems and could not be bothered to listen to Cushman and Carver. By the spring of 1618 they were not much further forward, and there was discouraging news. A group from the 'ancient church' of Amsterdam had also decided to cross the Atlantic and a party had actually set out for Virginia under their elder, Francis Blackwell. But the ship had been over-crowded, it had sailed late in the season, and the captain, Blackwell, and 130 out of the 180 in the ship were dead of dysentry and lack of fresh water before they reached Virginia. The letters between the Leyden people strive for Christian charity towards Blackwell, but it was not easy. He had split the church at Amsterdam, been arrested in London when seeking to arrange the crossing and obtained his freedom by betraying a comrade, and then by this ill-planned voyage queered the pitch of the Leyden men.

An odd friend at court for the Leyden men was Sir Edwin Sandys, son of the former Archbishop of York and the former landlord of the manor house at Scrooby. Sir Edwin, a determined Puritan, had been on the council of the Virginia Company for twelve years and when he became treasurer in 1619, Brewster himself, his former tenant, went to London with Cushman. As all attempts to get a patent in their own name had failed, a different approach was

Page 35 Southampton: (*above*) the West Gate through which John Alden and any other Pilgrims who joined the *Mayflower* and *Speedwell* in the port would have passed; (*left*) the Mayflower Memorial, with the funnel of the Cunard liner *Queen Elizabeth 2* clear in the background

Page 36 Dartmouth: (*above*) looking over the Mayflower Memorial to the harbour mouth and its guardian castle; (*below*) Bayard's Cove, the most likely point of the Pilgrim's departure

made. In June 1619 the Rev John Wincob, a sympathiser in the household of the Countess of Lincoln, received permission 'to plant himself and his associates' in Virginia; the idea, which never came off, was that he would go with the Leyden men. They were in any case in another kind of trouble.

A book from Brewster's press, the *Perth Assembly*, which attacked the king's religious policy in Scotland, gave great offence to King James. He made his ambassador in Holland demand the extradition of the printers and the destruction of the press. Brewer was in fact arrested and the type seized, but Brewster was not to be found. He was actually in England but by the time the hunt was raised for him there he had slipped away. To save the Dutch embarrassment, Brewer agreed voluntarily to go to England with a guarantee of a safe return; his examiners in London got little satisfaction from him and let him go back. One can judge the extent of the offence given by the book for, when Brewer moved back to England in 1626 he was thrown into prison and spent fourteen years there, until set free by the Long Parliament. Yet Brewster, for whom there were warrants out in England and Holland, and who had been the elder of the community since its move to Leyden, had already been chosen by the Leyden people as the man who would lead them into the New World. It had been realised that only a minority could cross the Atlantic in the first instance and Robinson was to stay behind with the majority and follow on later.

Now came new offers. The New Netherlands Company, which had claimed Manhattan and the Hudson River for Holland and had been trading there since 1614, offered to ship out John Robinson and 'the four hundred families'. They also petitioned the Prince of Orange for two warships to escort them and to see that the settlers were not molested by the English to the south, or the French who were already settled in Acadie, the modern Nova Scotia, to the north.

THE WESTON PLAN

At this time a new figure appeared on the scene, Thomas Weston. A London ironmonger, he was also selling cloth in Holland although this was strictly a business reserved to the Merchant Adventurers Company of London. His agent in Amsterdam, Edward

Pickering, was married to a member of the Leyden congregation and from him Weston no doubt heard of their plans to emigrate. He may have had religious sympathies with the Separatists, and had friends in the London business world who certainly did. At any rate he appeared in Leyden to put a new plan to the Englishmen there. He persuaded them not to rely overmuch on the Virginia Company, or to have anything to do with the Dutch, and proposed that he and a group of merchants in London should find the shipping and finance the venture. This was accepted and articles of agreement drawn up.

Weston's plan was a joint stock company with two kinds of shareholders, adventurers who would invest their money, and planters who would settle. Shares were in units of £10 ($24), each planter over the age of 16 would be given one share but could also invest, and all profits were to remain in the joint stock for seven years. At the end of that time the planters could keep the houses they had built, their goods, and the land they had tilled, for themselves, and all the rest, with the profits from trading and fishing, were to be divided proportionately among the shareholders. Each planter was to have two days of the week in which to work for himself.

In February 1620 one of the adventurers, John Pierce, got a patent for a plantation from the Virginia Company which named a tract of land near the mouth of the Hudson, at the very northern end of the London Company's land grant. All seemed set, but many of the Leyden people were disheartened. Some would not go at all, some were still for Virginia, some still hankered after Guiana even though Ralegh had come back empty-handed and been executed on Tower Hill. Against this, others in Leyden had already sold or mortgaged their property there to raise the money for the voyage, and could not turn back. To add to the confusion Weston now sought to amend the agreement. He struck out the clause giving each planter two days work for himself, and included all houses and land in the division to be made at the end of seven years.

This made the scheme more attractive to investors and brought in more adventurers, but the planters were strongly opposed. Four of them, Samuel Fuller, Edward Winslow, William Bradford and Isaac Allerton, wrote to Carver and Cushman, who were in England in May 1620 as their agents, protesting against these changes. Robinson was firmly on their side, and Cushman was told not to sign this new agreement. But Cushman wrote back that he and Weston already had a ship in mind for the voyage, the *Mayflower*, which had just discharged a cargo of French wine in London. Weston felt, and Cushman with him, that they had invested too much to turn back, and the Leyden people had already bought the *Speedwell*, a small craft, which they intended to keep on the coast after their arrival in the New World, for fishing and trading.

So they went ahead, with many misgivings, and to make up the number some planters from England were brought into the company. The newcomers appointed Christopher Martin of Billericay in Essex, who had links already with the Leyden congregation, as their agent. So Martin was busy in Kent getting provisions, Cushman and Weston were in London getting stores together, the Leyden people were equipping the *Speedwell* at Delftshaven, just outside Rotterdam, and Carver had gone to Southampton. That had been chosen as the port where the two bodies of planters, from Leyden and England, would join up.

So for the last time the Leyden congregation met together behind the Green Door, a 'day of solemn humilitation' Robinson called it, of prayers and tears and preaching. He urged those that were going, among other things, to shake off the name of Brownists, to close with the godly party of the Church of England, that is the Puritan branch, and to study union rather than division. He gave them advice on how they should run their affairs which they were long to remember.

> So they left the goodly and pleasante citie which had been ther resting place near 12 years; but they knew they were pilgrims and looked not much on these things, but lift up their eyes to ye heavens, their dearest cuntrie, and quieted their spirits.

When William Bradford wrote this account many years afterwards he appended a footnote, 'Heb 11'. In this Epistle to the Hebrews St Paul reminds them of all the trials their ancestors had endured for faith:

> . . . not having received the promises, but having seen them afar

off, and were persuaded of them, and embraced them, and confessed that they were strangers and pilgrims on the earth.

It is from this passage that later generations were to confer the name of the Pilgrim Fathers upon this little band.

From Leyden they went down the Vliet Canal, past the Hague and through Delft, past the flat fields and the dykes and the wind-mills of the country that had sheltered them for twelve years, to Delftshaven on the Maas. Most of the congregation at Leyden, and many friends from Amsterdam, accompanied them. With tears and prayers they made their farewells. They had endured much together already; now not only friends but families were being parted. John Robinson was saying goodbye to his sister, John Carver's wife; William Brewster and his wife were taking only the two youngest children; William Bradford and his wife were leaving their son John with the Robinsons. Some were destined never to meet again.

> But ye tide (which stays for no man) calling them away yt were thus loath to depart, their Reved pastor falling down on his knees (and they all with him) with watrie cheeks comended them with most fervente praiers to the Lord and his blessing.

So, on 22 July 1620, *Speedwell* sailed down the Maas, and the journey was under way.

CHAPTER THREE

False Starts

A FAIR WIND took *Speedwell* down through the Straits of Dover to reach Southampton in four days, on 26 July. *Mayflower* was waiting for her, having come round from the Thames a week before; in all likelihood the London people had joined *Mayflower* there and sailed round. Southampton as a meeting place saved *Speedwell* a time-wasting voyage up the Thames estuary and down again; it was also a quiet port where few questions were likely to be asked, and there were fewer royal officers to bother about this shipload of exiles from Holland.

The vast docks of modern Southampton, built out across the shallows of the rivers Itchen and Test, disguise the shape of the medieval town almost completely. In 1620 it stood at the junction of the rivers with the waters of the Test washing the stones of the west and south walls. Apart from small suburbs outside Bargate and Eastgate the town was still enclosed in the walls, which were at once its pride and its ruin. They had been built over two centuries earlier when the galleys of Venice and Florence, and the great carricks of Genoa, sailed into the port every year with all the riches of the Orient. Their crews had always stayed for several months before sailing home with the corn and wool of the rich counties around Southampton, so this trading brought much money into the town. Then the Italian cities had lost their monopoly of the Eastern trade to the Portuguese, and their ships came no longer to Southampton; exports now went through London, and by the early seventeenth century Southampton was in a considerable recession. Yet the town struggled to keep up the old walls, in spite of the cost and the less proud townsmen who pillaged them for stone to repair their own houses. To add to the town's problems, King James had just declared that he would not in future maintain Southampton Castle; no wonder that in 1620 the town was rent

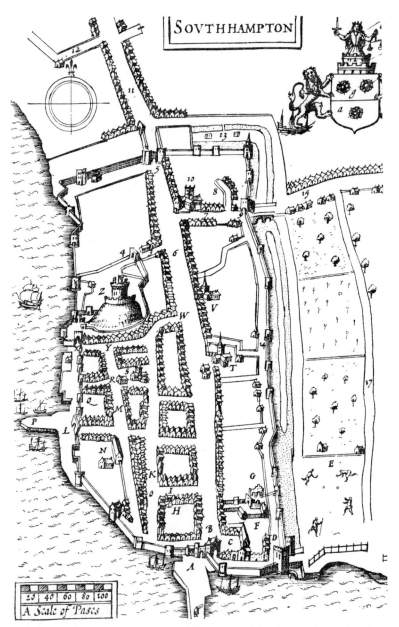

John Speed's 1611 map of Southampton. The letter *P* marks the West Quay, where *Mayflower* and *Speedwell* were anchored, and *L* the West Gate

with dissension. A petition to the town council that year com-
plained that the pavements were in disrepair, and the streets filthy.

Carver and Martin had ordered £700 ($1,666) worth of supplies
in the town for the voyage. Now, with the two ships anchored off
the West Quay, which was the commercial wharf, the business of
loading them, bringing the stores down through West Gate and
taking them out by boat, began. It was a hectic and unhappy
time. Cushman, Carver and Martin were at loggerheads over the
supplies. The arrivals from Leyden disapproved of the new agreement, which they said Cushman had no authority to accept on
their behalf. None of the adventurers came down to see the
planters before they sailed, apart from Weston. He brought down
the agreement for them to sign, and this they refused to do. Much
offended, he told them they must stand on their own feet and
would not advance another penny, though there was nearly £100
($238) owing in the town. To pay off their debts the company had
to sell £60 ($143) worth of their supplies, which left them perilously
short; little butter, no oil, not a sole to mend a shoe 'nor every man
a sword to his side, wanting many muskets, much armoure, &c.'

The passengers were divided among the two ships, and governors
and assistants appointed for each. Martin was given authority in
Mayflower with Cushman as his assistant; most of the senior Leyden
people stayed in *Speedwell*, to give confidence to her master,
Reynolds. There were already doubts about the smaller ship, and
she was trimmed twice at Southampton before they were ready
to sail. One new recruit was embarked there, a young cooper called
John Alden.

The two ships sailed on 5 August. The eleven days they had both
been at Southampton saw much heartache and, at sea, things
were not much better. In *Mayflower* Cushman and Martin were still
arguing about the finances, and Cushman found Martin overbear-
ing and high-handed. 'Friend, if ever we make a plantation, God
works a mirakle.' The sea was rough and Cushman very sick: 'Poore
William King & my self doe strive who shall be meate first for ye
fishes.' Things were even worse in *Speedwell*. '. . . shee is open
and leakie as a seive; and thr was a borde, a man might have puld
of with his fingers, 2 foote longe, wher ye water came in as at a
mole hole,' wrote Cushman, 'I thinke, as others also, if we had

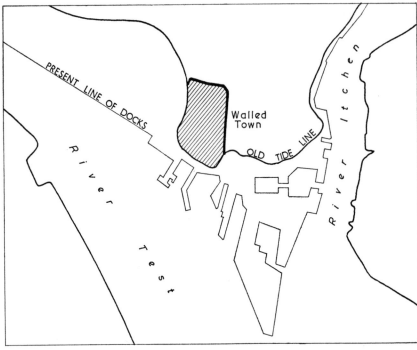

A sketch map of Southampton, showing the position of the walled
town the Pilgrims saw in relation to the modern shore line

stayed at sea but 3. or 4. howers more, shee would have sunke righte
downe.' Christopher Jones, the master, took *Mayflower* alongside
Speedwell to confer with Reynolds, and they decided to put into
Dartmouth, where they arrived on 13 August, six days out of
Southampton.

The little Devon town was enjoying a period of considerable
prosperity. The New Quay, now at the back of the boat pond,
had not long been built and fine gabled houses were going up along
its length. The south porch of St Saviour's, the parish church, was
being rebuilt, and within a few years the whole church was to be
rebuilt and extended. All this wealth came from the rich fishing
grounds off Newfoundland. This business had started soon after
the discovery of that territory by John Cabot in 1497, but not
until 1580, when the Danes began to restrict the use of the Ice-

landic fishing grounds, did the Newfoundland trade develop extensively, with the English driving off the French and Spanish fishermen. The west Channel ports were in the best position to exploit the new grounds, and Dartmouth took the lion's share with new men and merchants moving into the port to share the new prosperity. The ships would sail on 1 March, and not return home until late in the year.

So when *Speedwell* was in Dartmouth being repaired the fleet was away and the port quiet. The little ship was searched from stem to stern, and a few leaks dealt with. The workmen, Dartmouth shipwrights no doubt, pronounced themselves satisfied that she was in good order, and the two vessels sailed again, probably on 23 August.

But all was not well. Soon Reynolds was complaining that the *Speedwell* was making water faster than the pumps could clear her, and he must either go about or sink at sea. There was another consultation between the captains, and this time the two ships put into Plymouth. Bradford wrote many years later that they were 100 leagues, that is 300 miles, beyond Land's End when they had to turn back, but the time scale does not allow a round trip of 850 miles from Dartmouth out into the Atlantic and back to Plymouth. Captain John Smith wrote in 1622 that the leak developed the day after the two ships left Dartmouth, and this would make Plymouth the most convenient and logical port to use. But again in port no special leak could be found.

The general conclusion is that, in the refit to prepare the 60 ton *Speedwell* for the Atlantic crossing, she had been over-masted and was carrying too much sail. In harbour she was well enough; at sea with sail set the hull would work and open up, though after she had been sold and 'put into her old trime' she made many successful and profitable voyages. There were doubts among the passengers. The master and crew had been engaged to work for a year in the new plantation and the suspicion was that they had lost heart and wished to be free of the contract. It was thought too that the men were unhappy about the shortage of victuals, and could see themselves starving at sea while the *Mayflower*, carrying the bulk of the stores, would keep them for her own ship's company.

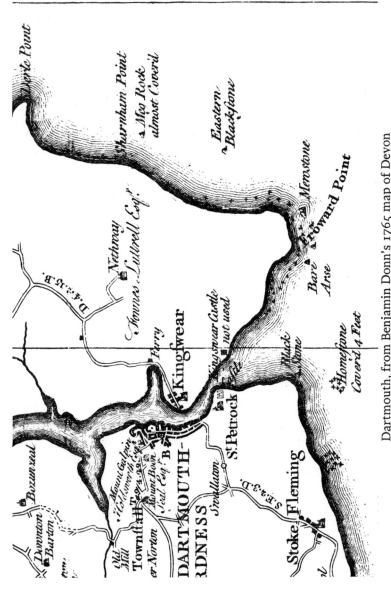

Dartmouth, from Benjamin Donn's 1765 map of Devon

At any rate it was decided in Plymouth to pay off *Speedwell*. Not everybody could go in one ship, but some of the would-be voyagers had also lost heart. Some felt too weak to face the ardours of the sea any longer, like Cushman and King who had been near death before even Dartmouth was reached. Others who went back were alarmed for their children, or discouraged by the constant delays and frustrations. About twenty dropped out and the remainder crowded into *Mayflower*, with what spare provisions that could be taken from *Speedwell*. Those abandoning the voyage joined *Speedwell* and went back to London in her; the remainder made ready once again for the Atlantic crossing. Apart from the officers and crew there were 102 passengers of whom 17 men, 10 women and 14 children were from the Leyden congregation. The English company also had 17 men but 9 women and 13 children. The servants included another woman and 6 children; 5 hired men completed the company.

Of the Leyden people only seven had been in the original Scrooby congregation : William Brewster and his wife, William Bradford, Francis Cooke, John Carver, and his wife Catherine and her brother William White from Sturton (John Robinson had married their sister). Other Leyden people were Isaac Allerton, Samuel Fuller (who took with him some knowledge of medicine and medical supplies), and Edward Winslow, who was joined by his younger brother Gilbert. In the English party were Stephen Hopkins, the only one who had been to the New World before, Christopher Martin, and Captain Miles Standish. He was a professional soldier who became the military leader of the colony and as a veteran of the Dutch wars he may not have been a stranger to the Leyden people. In his will he left a legacy to Mercy Robinson 'whom I tenderly love for her grandfather's sake'. If that means the Rev John Robinson, Standish must have known him in Leyden, for he certainly could not have met him after 1620.

At long last *Mayflower* was ready to sail. The first history of the Pilgrims, the *New England's Memorial* written in 1669 by Nathaniel Morton, William Bradford's nephew, contains the words:

This name of Plymouth was so called . . . because Plymouth in old England was the last town they left in their native country and for that they received many kindnesses from some Christians there.

No comment, favourable or unfavourable, is made by any of the contemporary writers on the other English ports touched at, though *Mayflower* was in Southampton for about 18 days, in Dartmouth for 10 days, and Plymouth for 14 days. Both Dartmouth and Plymouth were unplanned calls, but it is fitting that Plymouth should have been the final point of departure. No other town in Britain had played so big a part in opening the Americas, no other community could understand quite so completely what these people were facing, and many of them were in sympathy with the religious outlook of the Pilgrims.

PLYMOUTH AND THE PROTESTANTS

Plymouth had a long Protestant tradition. It had had to fight the monks of Plympton to win municipal independence. It had stood aloof from the first Cornish rebellion in defence of the Old Faith, and stuck the head of the rebel leader on a pole over its Guildhall, only to see the Guildhall burnt by the Cornish when they rose a second time. Its seamen had taken letters of marque from the Prince of Condé and the Prince of Orange, leaders of the Huguenots of France and the Protestants of Holland, to harry Spain at sea. So many privateers of all three nations had used the port as a base that its quays had been extended to cope with them; it was fighting Protestant England's war against Catholic Europe before Queen Elizabeth was convinced that it was a national necessity.

Plymouth merchants were the first Englishmen to trade across the Atlantic; when they tried to take part in the Caribbean trade of the Spanish colonies they had met treachery and deceit, had seen their seamen burnt at the stake or sent to the galleys. The seaman may be no puritan in the moral sense of that word but he lives constantly exposed to death, and is accustomed to praying to his God without the intermediate help of a priest, so the nonconforming ideas were suited to his outlook.

The town had been given the right to appoint its own vicars by

Queen Elizabeth in 1572. It also paid for lecturers, the preachers, and from 1608 onwards it is clear that Plymouth was appointing well-known Puritans. There was a nest of such parsons around the town with several men of national repute; one can only assume that they were far enough from the centres of authority to escape the fate of their brothers around Scrooby.

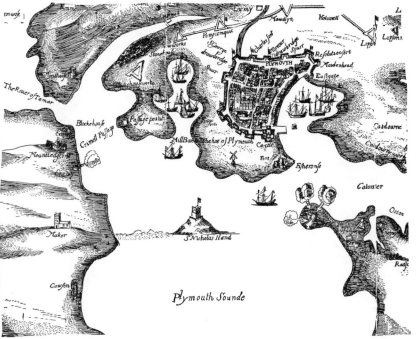

Plymouth in 1643, a detail from the 'Siege Map' made during the Civil War. *Mayflower* sailed from Sutton Pool, east of the town

These views were not confined to the priesthood. In 1607 the Rev Samuel Heiron of Modbury, a few miles from Plymouth, published a fierce protest against clergymen being hounded out of their church because they would not conform to the Prayer Book. It was printed secretly in Holland, smuggled into Plymouth in the goods of the most prominent merchant of the day, and scattered about the streets and 'on the doorsteps of scholars' so that people could find it. The smuggler was Thomas Sherwell, mayor three times, and member of Parliament for the town from 1614 until his death in 1631, when a distinguished Puritan preached at his funeral. He supervised the building of the Guildhall which Plymouth started in 1606 out of its new prosperity and, with his brother Nicholas, built and largely paid for the Orphan's Aid, a children's home beside the parish church. Nicholas Sherwell was mayor the year before the Pilgrims arrived; Thomas Fownes was in office when they were in the port and Robert Rawlyn followed him; all were generous donors to the Orphan's Aid and other almshouses built at this time. Much charitable work was being done; faith and good works were going hand-in-hand.

Apart from the merchants the landed gentry were Puritan sympathisers, for the published sermons of the Puritans are dedicated to many of them and these writers preached at their funerals. It is not without significance that of the great leaders of Parliament in the struggles against the Stuart kings which culminated in the Civil War, Eliot, Strode and Pym were all close neighbours of Plymouth.

The Civil War undoubtedly brought to Plymouth, among the Parliamentary troops who garrisoned the town for the war-long siege against the Royalists, Nonconformists of all shapes. Both parish churches, the old St Andrew's and the new Charles (which Plymouth had fought for when King Charles forced a High Church priest into St Andrew's) were holding Presbyterian services during the war, and there was a Baptist congregation of 150 by 1648. Old George Street Baptist Church in modern Plymouth is in direct descent from that church, and claims an even earlier foundation, believing that its members were the 'Christians' who entertained the Pilgrims. It is possible; a branch in London of the 'ancient church' of Amsterdam was openly meeting at Southwark by 1616 and is now remembered by the Pilgrim Father's Memorial Church there. There may well have been such a congregation in Plymouth at that time, which had regular shipping links with London and Holland. On the other hand the apparent freedom of St Andrew's to pursue an advanced Puritan course at that time gave little cause for separation. The Corporation had appointed the Rev Henry Wallis as vicar in 1603, and the sermon preached at his funeral in 1633 shows clearly that he was as Puritan as his lecturers.

PLYMOUTH AND THE AMERICAN EXPLORATIONS

But apart from a common ground with the Pilgrims in religion, Plymouth people were also deeply interested in their destination. Apart from the early trading across the Atlantic, the first attempt to plant an English colony in America had been made from Plymouth. Sir Walter Ralegh, the moving spirit behind the 1585 settlement at Roanoke, an island off the modern North Carolina, sent his cousin Sir Richard Grenville to lead the expedition. Sir Richard sailed from Plymouth with a number of Plymouth men, including the second-in-command, among the colonists. The expedition failed, like the second Roanoke venture two years later, largely because support ships did not get through quickly enough with supplies, but in all likelihood Spain would have destroyed the colony in the same way as she had wiped out the French Huguenot settlement in Carolina in 1567.

The Roanoke failures, and their high cost, deterred such adventures for some years, but early in the next century three English parties all with Plymouth links, and a French expedition, explored the North American coast. Bartholomew Gosnold planted an English settlement just south of Cape Cod in 1602 but it only survived one winter. Champlain had better fortune, he did establish a French settlement on the Bay of Fundy in 1604. George Weymouth in 1605 took home five Indians whom he gave to Sir Ferdinando Gorges, governor of Plymouth Fort. His imagination was stirred and he too plunged into the speculative efforts to found an American colony. Two charters were granted by King James that year, one to the London Company of Virginia and the other to the Plymouth Company of Virginia.

Gorges, Chief Justice Popham, Ralegh Gilbert (the heir to the Ralegh patent for Virginia) and several Plymouth merchants formed the Plymouth Company. Their first ship was captured by the Spanish and so the London Company established the first colony, at Jamestown, in 1607. In May of that year another Plymouth venture went out with Ralegh Gilbert as admiral, George Popham as president, and two of Gorges's Indians as guides. They set up Fort St George, at the mouth of the Kennebec in Maine. Relief ships came out the next spring to tell Gilbert that his elder brother had died and that he must come home to administer the family estates. Old George Popham had died in the Maine winter, and the rest of the company would not remain without leaders. So another colony from Plymouth failed.

Jamestown succeeded. They had Gosnold to help their early planning, and then the bullying drive of Captain John Smith, a veteran of the Dutch wars, to carry them through. It was a long uphill struggle but it became the first English colony in North America and by accident the founder of the Bermuda settlement when the flagship of the 1609 supply fleet from Plymouth was wrecked on the island. The men wintered there and went back as colonists. The Spanish, now past the zenith of their power, interfered with neither Jamestown nor Bermuda, though they threatened once or twice. Indeed the English were now feeling their power, and in 1613 the Virginians expelled the French from two of their settlements. The expulsion was not complete, for the French were well spread across the modern Nova Scotia and New Brunswick, and had already reached up to the St Lawrence.

Between the English and the French the Dutch moved in, trading with the Indians on the river which the English navigator Henry Hudson had explored and named in 1609. Then Captain John Smith, out of Virginia after a gunpowder accident, explored the northern coast in 1614 and became convinced that this was the place for English settlers. He published an enthusiastic account and christened the land New England. On his map the principal features were named by his patron Prince Charles (afterwards King Charles I), but of the royal names only Charles River, Cape Ann, and Plymouth are still in use. His was not the first map of the coast, nor was it the first name given to this new Plymouth. Martin Pring from Devon had called it Whitson (or Whitesand) Bay in 1603 when he stayed there for seven weeks; Champlain made a harbour plan in 1605 and called it Port du Cap St Louis; a Dutchman named it Cranes Bay in 1614 and Henry F. Howe, the American historian, speculates on whether the Pilgrims could have seen his map in Holland when they were debating emigration.

A third visitor to this Plymouth of many names in 1614 was Thomas Hunt, in one of Smith's ships, who took twenty Indians prisoner and sold them as slaves in Spain for £20 ($48) each.

Page 53 Plymouth: The carved granite in the pavement of the west pier of Sutton Harbour marks, within a few paces, the actual spot from which the Pilgrims sailed, and the bronze tablet framed by the canopy records that they had been 'kindly entertained and courteously used by divers friends there dwelling'

Page 54 Plymouth: (*above*) a party of American tourists rejoin their bus by the Mayflower Stone; the Pilgrims are thought to have slept in Island House, the white building behind the left corner of the monument; (*below*) Sutton Harbour

Another ship that year, sent by Gorges to trade for furs, got into a major battle with the Indians south of Cape Cod, and these two events turned the coast Indians into bitter enemies of English visitors. From this same exposure to Europeans the Indians contracted some disease, probably a child's ailment like measles, against which they had no immunity, and in a few years the population was decimated.

Smith in England was trying to stir the members of the old Plymouth Company into action. They found some ships for him in 1615, and though Smith himself was captured by French privateers (everything happened to John Smith), four others made the voyage and came home well stocked with fish and furs—beaver, otter, martin, black fox and sable. So from then on each summer, Popham, Trelawny, Gorges and other Plymouth merchants sent ships to New England which set up small trading posts ashore at which to buy furs. The new Plymouth got a new name when some Indians stole from the trading post there; the men rechristened it Thievish Harbour. The fishermen normally used islands as their bases, they were safer. They referred to the coast proper as Maine, the mainland, just as their predecessors in the Caribbean had called South America the Spanish Main. These summer voyages yielded quick profits and few risks; in 1619 one Plymouth ship of 200 tons, with a crew of thirty-eight, was on the coast for six weeks and sold its cargo for £2,000 ($4,760). It paid more than the Newfoundland fishing; a seaman there made £6-£7 ($14-$17) a season; for a New England voyage his share was £14 ($33).

One of Gorges's captains on the coast in 1619 was Thomas Dermer. He called at Newfoundland on the way and there found an Indian called Squanto, whom he had met the year before, one of those who had been taken prisoner in 1614 at the new Plymouth and sold into Spain. By some means he had got to London, lived for a few years with a merchant there, and in time got back to Newfoundland. Now Dermer took him as pilot for his New England voyage. In Massachusetts Bay and the new Plymouth they found formerly populous places quite empty, and the plague still rampant. From new Plymouth Squanto took Dermer west to what is now the Taunton River where he met two chiefs, and the Englishman established friendly relations with them. Squanto stayed behind.

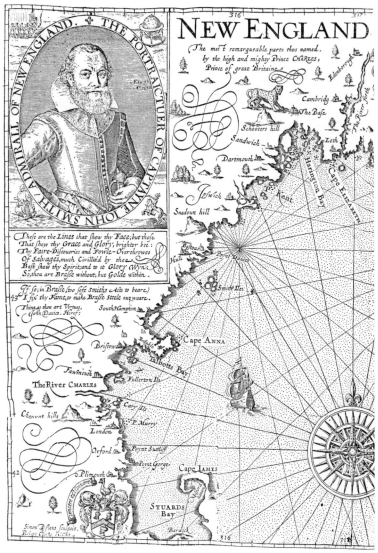

Part of Captain John Smith's map of New England, with the names which the Prince of Wales, later King Charles I, bestowed upon the prominent features. Plymouth appears just above the Smith coat of arms at the foot, but the house drawn there, like all the others, is merely a device of the cartographer

Smith in England was still arguing that settlement, not quick trading trips, was the real way to tap the wealth of America. He convinced Gorges, who set to work with national instead of local figures to revive the Plymouth Company and a new charter was secured by them in 1620. Gorges with his Puritan sympathies and intense interest in America must have known all about the Pilgrims when they arrived in old Plymouth. Certainly Captain John Smith did. He said he had offered to go as their captain but they took his book and map instead as being cheaper—the book was still in William Brewster's library at his death. Miles Standish had the post Smith wanted; Standish was fiery enough, but to think of Smith with all his braggadocio serving with the Pilgrims is too much.

The summer that *Mayflower* and *Speedwell* anchored in old Plymouth there were eight ships from the port on the New England coast, and perhaps forty or fifty fishing off Newfoundland. Every family in the town would have had some of their men away with those ships; they all lived in a tight little community round Sutton Harbour. They would have seen the Pilgrims' ships, heard their story, known that the end of August was too late to be setting out across the Atlantic and that their own men would soon be homeward bound. Given religious sympathies as well, it is little wonder that they offered comfort and succour to these already battered travellers.

PILGRIM'S VIEW OF PLYMOUTH

The Pilgrim ship would have sailed in under the Hoe, past Fisher's Nose with the new fort on top which Francis Drake had built and which Gorges now commanded. It had superseded the medieval fort above the narrows of the harbour entrance, which had reverted to a military store. In front of it a stubby pier projected in front of the Barbican, or watergate, where a winch operated a chain which could be lifted to keep out enemy ships. Beside the pier new stone steps led down to the water's edge. Just north was the causey, a stone causeway running out over the mud to low-water mark, and beyond that the new quay of 1570 built for the Protestant privateers. Facing this quay were new, brightly-painted, Elizabethan houses, their upper storeys leaning forward. Narrow little streets, all built in the recent prosperity, led off from this quay and from Southside Street, the way to the old town. One of the streets, called New Street still, had just been built by John Sparke who as a young man had sailed with John Hawkins to the Indies and wrote the first English descriptions of tobacco and the potato. No 32 New Street is a showpiece now; old deeds call it London House and it may have been the Plymouth offices of the London Company of Virginia.

The west and north sides of the harbour, apart from the new quay (which is all now called the Barbican), were lined with warehouses which came right to the water's edge. The eastern side was little developed, and on the mud there it is most likely that *Speedwell* was beached and examined; *Mayflower* probably stayed at anchor under the castle. There is a legend that some of the Pilgrims slept ashore in the attics of Island House, one of the old houses still overlooking the harbour. It is also claimed that some slept in Hawker's wine cellars, on the north side. Certainly Island House was as near *Mayflower* as could be, and convenient. If *Speedwell* was berthed on the eastern mud then Hawker's cellars would have been the nearest building. Quite likely all the passengers came ashore for *Speedwell* to be searched; when the changeover of those who were going on and those going back was made the ships probably laid side by side. Nevertheless it would have been a godsend to spend a few nights ashore, both the London and the Leyden companies having been cooped up in their cramped quarters for a month by the time they got to Plymouth.

What stories of America, the unknown land, could their hosts have told them? Tobacco, New England fish and furs, were all familiar commodities. Indians had been seen in and out of the port since old William Hawkins brought the first one home from Brazil in 1532. The most recent visitor had been the Princess Pocohontas who as a small girl had pleaded with her father to spare Captain John Smith's life in Virginia; she had arrived in 1616 with her tobacco-planter husband, John Rolfe. Negro servants, men and women, were commonplace. For people who had been living a sheltered life in Leyden, far from the sea, this must have seemed indeed the edge of the unknown.

When, in time, they crossed the ocean and settled in this strange New World, they had John Smith's map to tell them their new home was called Plymouth, but they could look back to the old Plymouth and remember it as their last contact with the known, familiar, civilised life. To have been ashore in England once more after such years of exile in the Netherlands must have stirred the emotions. Edward Winslow opened the narrative of *Mourt's Relation*, the first account of the colony and printed in 1622, with the words:

Wednesday, the sixth of September, the wind coming east-north-west, a fine small gale, we loosed from Plymouth, having been kindly entertained and courteously used by divers friends there dwelling. . . .

That, in his mind, written within the twelvemonth, was the start, the opening moment, of the whole great adventure.

CHAPTER FOUR

Ship, Voyage and Landfall

MAYFLOWER WAS A COMMON enough name for ships of this period, though no one can be quite sure what flower is meant. Contemporary references make it both the lily-of-the-valley and the cowslip; it may even have been the Tudor rose, which would explain its popularity. Now it is generally assumed to be the flower of the hawthorn, whose little five-petalled white flowerlets clustering over a tree until they look like snow in sunshine are still as much part of the scent and scene of the more rustic corners of England as the dogwood is in the New England forests. Country people in England still call the hawthorn 'may blossom'; it is said that in the New World the same name was used for the similar flowers of the trailing arbutus, which since 1918 has been the official flower of Massachusetts.

Equally no one can be sure which of the *Mayflowers* in the port registers of the time is the Pilgrim ship. Three, for instance, appear in the old Plymouth port books for 1620, but not the Pilgrim ship because she landed no cargo. She may have been the 200 ton *Mayflower*, commanded by Edward Banks, which was 'set forth and paid upon the charge of the city of London' for the Armada fighting in 1588. One of that *Mayflower's* owners was John Vassal. In 1591 Vassal moved from Ratcliffe, in the parish of Stepney (on the north banks of the Thames, below London Bridge) to Leigh-on-Sea at the mouth of the estuary. In 1606 the *Mayflower* of Leigh was loading cloth in London for Middelburgh; in 1607 the *Mayflower* of London was unloading wine from Gascony. Port registration was very haphazard in those days, but a Robert Bonner of Leigh was her master in both years, and a Christopher Jones appears in both years as master of the *Josan*. In 1608 Bonner appears as master of the *Josan*, and the next year Jones was master of the *Mayflower*—a switch of ships seems a reasonable assumption. Jones was also quarter-owner of the *Mayflower*. He was born at Maldon and married at Harwich, which accounts for a suggestion that *Mayflower* was a Harwich ship.

In 1611 Jones moved to Rotherhithe to live, in Southwark on the south bank of the Thames. It was a village then; forty years later Samuel Pepys used to walk to the Half Way House there to gather cowslips beside the river and once remarked on a pretty girl he saw in a little lane running out into the fields. But it was, as it still is, part of the port of London, and from this time forwards *Mayflower* is always described as of London. Maritime historians are reasonably certain that this is the Pilgrim ship; of the earlier clues tracing her back to Armada days they will say no more than that they make the link probable.

Her voyages from 1609 onwards can be traced through the port books, all short-voyage trading. Normally she would sail with cargoes of cloth and stockings, sometimes with rabbit skins as well, and once with tobacco, to La Rochelle, the Charente river and Bordeaux, all on the west coast of France, and return with cognac and wine. The only breaks in the pattern are a 1609 voyage to Norway and two 1614 voyages to Hamburg, taking out English cloth and bringing home taffetas, satins and similar fabrics. On 23 May 1620 she had just completed her second voyage of the year to the French coast and was unloading cognac and wine from La Charente, when she was chartered by Weston for the Atlantic crossing.

Writing to Leyden, Cushman called her a fine ship, though he had some doubts as to whether she was big enough. The only alternatives, he said, were too large. Probably *Mayflower* was as big as they could afford. Two of the adventurers had shipped goods in her before and presumably considered her, in spite of age and size, as being fit for an Atlantic crossing. A ship of 180 tons which rounded Ushant all the year round could be expected to face the north Atlantic in summer without trouble. The ships which old Plymouth had been sending to New England for some years past were all about the same size.

As master and part-owner, Christopher Jones probably managed the ship as well, using Rotherhithe as the home port. It would be reasonable to look to the village, an important part of the port of

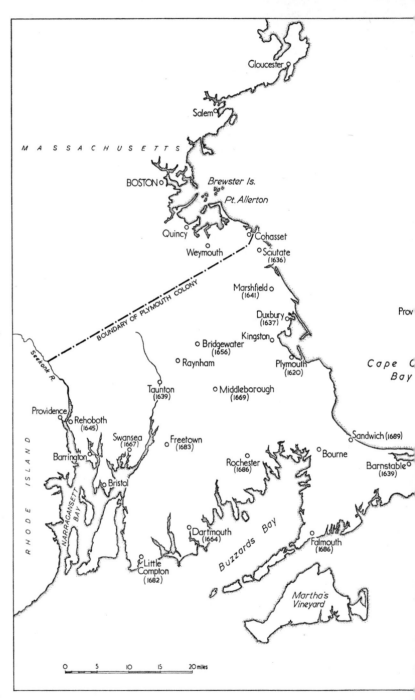

Sketch-map of Plymouth Colony; the dates in parenthesis
enlargement of the Cape Cod area showing ap

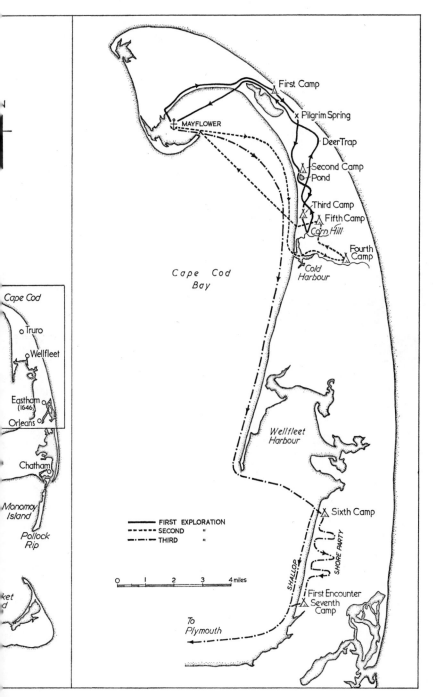

Labels within the map:

First Camp

x Pilgrim Spring

MAYFLOWER

Deer Trap

Second Camp
Pond

Third Camp
Fifth Camp
Corn Hill

Fourth Camp

Cold Harbour

Cape Cod Bay

Wellfleet Harbour

Sixth Camp

SHORE PARTY

SHALLOP

First Encounter
Seventh Camp

To Plymouth

Inset map (left):

Cape Cod

o Truro

o Wellfleet

Eastham (1646)

Orleans

Chatham

Monomoy Island

Pollock Rip

Legend:

——— FIRST EXPLORATION
- - - SECOND "
-·-·- THIRD "

0   1   2   3   4 miles

hen the various settlements were recognised as towns. *Right,* an
ately the early wanderings of the Pilgrim explorers

Mayflower II with the shallop alongside, a Plimoth Plantation drawing

London, for the other officers and men. The first mate, John Clark, who had already made two crossings to Jamestown, came from a family which lived at Clark's Orchard in Rotherhithe, and he was baptised and married in the parish church. The Rector since 1611, the Rev Thomas Gataker, was a Puritan and had just been travelling in Holland to study Dutch Protestantism, which he feared was imperilled by the foreign policy of James I. At Southwark, just a mile up the river, the Separatists had been meeting openly since 1616. None of this necessarily makes the *Mayflower* officers and crew into Puritans or Nonconformists, but they would have been acquainted with the motives of their Pilgrim passengers.

Of the second mate, John Coppin, it is only known that he had been on the New England coast once before, the only one in the whole ship's company, as far as can be told. Captain John Smith was very critical of the fact that 'for want of experience' the Pilgrims ranged about for six weeks before finding a place to settle, but he was the rejected leader, and always in two minds about the expedition. He approved the project in general and the financing by 'some well-disposed gentlemen of London and other places', which was not dissimilar to that of Jamestown and Bermuda, but disliked the 'leaking unwholesome ship'.

All we know of *Mayflower* from Pilgrim writings is that she was 'of burden about 9. score', which is taken to mean 180 tons. Even her name only slips into one document casually. What we know about her history was built up by Dr J. W. Horrocks in a series of articles in the *Mariner's Mirror* during 1922. Dr R. C. Anderson, a founder of the National Maritime Museum at Greenwich and of the Society for Nautical Research, worked on this material when asked in 1926 to design the model which is now in Pilgrim Hall at Plymouth, Mass.

This scholarship was the starting-point of the work of Mr William A. Baker, the American naval architect and Curator of the Francis Russell Hart Nautical Museum in the Massachusetts Institute of Technology, when he designed *Mayflower II*. She is the actual size, and as close to the original *Mayflower* as possible in every respect. Mr Baker's greatest guide in the end was the note-book of his namesake, Matthew Baker, now in Magdalene College Library, Cambridge, which contains a number of ship profiles and working drawings of the master shipwright who was producing England's best ships in late Elizabethan times, when *Mayflower* was probably built. *Mayflower II*, built by Uphams of Brixham in Devon and sailed across to Plymouth, Mass, in 1957 by Captain Alan Villiers, is as near as scholarship is ever likely to take us to the original. She is 183 tons by the rule of 1582, by modern measurement 220 tons net and 365 tons displacement; 104 ft long overall and 79 ft on the waterline, with 25 ft beam and drawing 12 ft 6 in when fully laden, with a freeboard of 6 ft 8 in. Suggestions that she is cocked up too high in the stern are countered by looking at contemporary English and Dutch maritime paintings; the ship in Captain John Smith's map (page 56) for instance is even more high-sterned. On her maindeck Mr Baker allowed enough room under the beams for the tens of thousands of visitors she has each year to walk through without accident, but the actual clearance

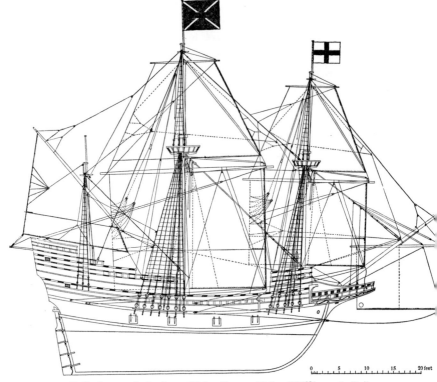

Sail plan and rigging of *Mayflower II*, by William A. Baker

under the beams is fully justified by surviving seventeenth-century
accounts and drawings of ships.

The Pilgrims had a shallop, a small open craft propelled by sail
or oars, which they cut down and stowed on the main deck of
Mayflower for use on the coast. Again a full scale reproduction
has been designed by Mr Baker and built by Plymouth Marine Railways Incorporated of Plymouth, Massachusetts. This type of craft
is even more obscure than the ship itself, but the Pilgrim records
show that their boat carried sail on one mast, eighteen men with
food, arms and equipment on one trip and thirty-two on another.
Again Mr Baker researched the problem in America, in England,
and in other European museums and libraries. His reproduction, as

sound a working boat as *Mayflower II*, is 33 ft 3 in × 9 ft 2 in with a draught of 3 ft 3 in, with leeboards. She is too big to stow in *Mayflower II* but the Pilgrims had to have their shallop cut down for the Atlantic crossing. How this was done is guesswork. Mr Baker's view is that the top few planks were removed on each side and the ribs cut off, and in Provincetown Harbour, where the Pilgrim carpenter took over two weeks to rebuild her, the ribs were extended again by scarfing, or extra ribs fastened alongside, and the planking restored.

In *Mayflower* the captain would have been berthed in the small cabin on the after end of the half-deck. The other two officers and the crew of about twenty men would have to find accommodation somewhere, but if the Pilgrims had all the great cabin, 25 ft × 15 ft at its greatest beam, and the main deck, 75 ft × 20 ft, there would have been 102 men, women and children to pack into less than 1,800 sq ft, without allowing for the shallop, the windlass, and all the other ship's gear. It works out at about 18 sq ft each, say an area 6 ft × 3 ft, the space of one modern single bed, for each person. That is an over-estimate, but in that they had to live. 'Add cold weather, cold water dripping down on all through leaking decks and topsides, and toss liberally around the north Atlantic for two months', writes Mr Baker in *The New Mayflower, her Building and Construction* 'and one cannot but admire the courage and fortitude of the little band.'

Probably they slept, whole families together, in their own blankets and on their own straw mattresses, on the bare decks. They had victualled collectively, and what little cooking they could do was by families on the little brick oven in the fore-peak, or on charcoal stoves in the tiller flat. They were so crowded that some even slept in the shallop. The time from leaving Leyden to the final move ashore in New England must have seemed interminable; 47 days before they left Plymouth, 66 days on the Atlantic crossing, and another 131 days before the last settlers went to live ashore—244 days or 8 months.

THE VOYAGE

The direct route from old Plymouth to Cape Cod is 2,800 nautical miles but entails an adverse current and head winds. It is used by small yachts in the modern single-handed transatlantic race but these fore-and-aft craft go to windward much more efficiently than the old square-riggers. Alan Villiers found that *Mayflower II* would make up to six points on the wind, which is a better performance than one would have expected, but he took the southern route that sailormen have used for centuries, down to the Canaries on the north-east trade winds, and then picking up the south-east trades. Apart from fair winds it uses the north Atlantic currents to full advantage, but gave Villiers a passage of 5,420 nautical miles and took him fifty-one days. He found the ship would ghost well in light winds, make seven knots regularly in good winds, and ride bad weather under bare poles comfortably. She made 164 miles on her best day, and her average day's sailing of 106 miles compared very well with that of the big craft of the last great days of sailing ships.

Alan Villiers made a summer passage, Christopher Jones a late autumn crossing; against that Villiers had to learn to handle a wooden ship with rope rigging as he went, Jones had been master of *Mayflower* for eleven years by 1620. His ship was more heavily laden, and he took sixty-six days. His route can only be guessed; Plymouth men of his time were familiar with the southern route but equally the shortest northern route, nearly great-circle sailing, to Newfoundland and then down the American coast, was well used. The third alternative is to sail south-west to the Azores on the same latitude as Cape Cod, and then west, and this may well have been the route Jones used. The Pilgrims were not seamen and they leave us no clues, but this was a route used by contemporary seamen bound for New England or Virginia.

Bradford tells us that *Mayflower* had a fair wind for several days after she sailed from Plymouth, which was some encouragement though many of the Pilgrims were seasick, and clearly not for the first time. One lusty young seaman cursed and mocked them in their misery and kept declaring that he hoped to help cast half of them overboard before their journey's end. There is a smug satisfaction in Bradford's record that in fact it was this arrogant youngster who, before half the voyage, was himself smitten with disease and buried at sea, 'ye just hand of God upon him'.

The fair weather did not last. They met head winds and fierce storms which severely shook the ship. She began to work in the heavy weather and opened her decks, so that all their sleeping quarters were constantly wet. A main beam amidship cracked under the strain and bent, so that they feared for the safety of the ship and debated with the officers whether they should run for England rather than battle on. But Jones assured them that the ship was strong and firm under water, and with the aid of a great iron screw that the Pilgrims had brought from Holland the beam was jacked back into position and secured with a post from the lower deck wedged under it. There has been speculation that the screw was part of the Leyden printing press; otherwise it is hard to account for so odd a piece of equipment in the Pilgrim luggage.

The decks were caulked, though the sleeping quarters remained wetter than they had been before, and by not carrying too much sail *Mayflower* held on. She still met storms which she could only ride under bare poles, with not a stitch of sail set, and in one such storm young John Howland, a member of John Carver's household, was swept off the deck. He grabbed the topsail halliards, which were hanging over the side, and was eventually hauled back in board: 'Though he was something ill with it, yet he lived many years after, and became a profitable member both in church and comone wealthe.' Only one passenger died in the voyage, young William Butten from Austerfield, a servant of Samuel Fuller. In these conditions Elizabeth Hopkins gave birth to a son, who was fittingly enough christened Oceanus.

At daybreak on 9 November, in fair wind and weather, they at last made a landfall, and 'were not a little joyful'. It was Cape Cod and, after some consultation among themselves and with Captain Jones, they decided to stand to the south and the Hudson River, where their patent gave them the right to settle. By midday they 'fell among deangerous shoulds and roring breakers', to this day a fair description of Pollock Rip over the shoals below Monomoy Island at the southern corner of Cape Cod. The wind was turning foul and weakening; to see land after so long and then sail away from it into new dangers was too much. Once again the ship changed course, back for Cape Cod, and on 11 November *Mayflower* was quietly at anchor in Provincetown Harbour.

Much play has been made of a story, not published for forty

years, that Captain Jones had been bribed by the Dutch to keep the Pilgrims away from their settlement on the Hudson. None of the earlier accounts, written by people who were aboard *Mayflower* and knew Jones, give any hint of this. It would have needed fast work by the Dutchmen, because Jones was only approached about the voyage in the second week of June and he sailed for Southampton a month later. There were times when Jones was anxious to get the Pilgrims ashore, once he reached New England, and be off; there were irritations between him and his passengers; but all natural and understandable, and one can find in the Pilgrim writings a number of instances of his kindliness and friendship.

The Pilgrim leaders knew they had turned their back on the place where they had a lawful right to settle; that north of the Cape was in the patent of the Council for New England who might give trouble. There was trouble too nearer at hand, for if they settled where they had no lawful authority they had no right to elect leaders or make laws. Some of the 'strangers', the Englishmen who had joined the Leyden people at Southampton, were aware of this, and declared 'that when they came ashore they would use their owne libertie; for none had power to comand them. . . .' Some of the leaders, after the first prayers for their safe arrival, therefore drew up what has come to be known as the Mayflower Compact, in which they all agreed to combine into a civil body politic, to frame laws and appoint officers, and to which all promised submission and obedience.

John Carver was elected the first governor; he had many claims to the position. As a merchant from Doncaster, ten miles up the Great North Road from Scrooby, he was probably one of the original company, and was a man of substance who had sunk most of his considerable fortune into the enterprise, probably more than any other planter. He had been the leading spirit in the emigration from Leyden, and was employed in the London negotiations because of his knowledge of the world. Although he upbraided Cushman for negligence, he also strove to keep the peace between him and the others. Apart from Brewster he was probably the eldest of the company, and his wife's younger sister was John Robinson's wife. He had been the first to sign the compact, followed by Bradford, Winslow, Brewster, Allerton, Standish, Alden, Fuller, Martin

Page 71 The *Mayflower II* at sea off the American coast in a strong wind. The fore topsail has been taken in and the main topsail is being furled, but she is sailing very close to the wind for a square-rigged ship. Apart from making the Atlantic crossing, this full-sized reproduction of the Pilgrim ship has sailed south from Plymouth, Mass, to New York and Florida, and 'down east' to Maine

Page 72 Rotherhithe, home port of *Mayflower*: (*above*) looking up the Thames from the terrace of the Angel Inn to Tower Bridge; (*left*) the parish church of St Mary's in whose churchyard, now a children's playground, the master, Christopher Jones, was buried; (*below*) the Mayflower Inn across the road from the church, which also looks over the river and sells English and United States postage stamps, as well as beer, across the bar

and Mullins. Already these men were establishing themselves as the leaders. In all, forty-one people signed the compact, the head of each household. It was a document based on the form used by the Separatists to bind themselves together into a church, adapted now for political purposes. It has been hailed as the first declaration of democracy on American soil; really it was a simple method of ensuring unity in a dangerous land.

CAPE COD

Cape Cod had been so christened by Gosnold, because of the plentiful supply of fish there. They still were in evidence, though the Pilgrims lacked the means of catching them. John Smith had described the place as 'only a headland of high hills of sand overgrown with shrubby pines, hurts (cranberries) and such trash'. The barren soil and strange geographical shape are both explained by the geological formation. In the last Ice Age the continental ice sheet had pushed down over the area, carrying millions of tons of boulders and sand in its leading edge. As in time it melted and shrank back again the debris was dropped, forming first the east-west ridge of which the islands of Nantucket and Martha's Vineyard alone remain, then the parallel ridge which is the southernmost part of Cape Cod. As the ice melted, the rivers from Maine came down over the ice, carving deep valleys which were filled with more granite sand, and when the ice finally disappeared these north-south deposits were left forming the outer arm of the Cape, and the strange sand ridges of Plymouth Beach and Duxbury Beach on the other side of Cape Cod Bay. The currents of the sea, and the waves, were left to make more changes that still go on through the centuries. By no means could it be called a fertile land. No wonder that Bradford wrote:

> What could they see but a hidious & desolate wildernes, full of wild beasts & wild men? . . . For summer being done, all things stand upon them with a wetherbeaten face; and ye whole countrie, full of woods & thickets, represented a wild & savage heiw.

E

73

Behind them was the ocean, cutting them off from home and friends.

But there is always hope. The men who went ashore in the ship's longboat on the Saturday that the compact was signed said the soil was good black earth a spade's depth thick; they brought back juniper for their fires. Sunday, as always with the Pilgrims, was a day of rest and prayer; on Monday the women went ashore to wash their clothes and the men got the shallop to the beach to build her up again. They found that the harbour was very shallow, even from the longboat they had a long wade. In the freezing cold of November many of them soon had colds and coughs, and the mussels they found on the beach made them sick. The ship had to anchor nearly a mile off-shore; this was no place to unload stores or to settle.

People sleeping in the shallop had strained and opened the seams, and it was clearly going to take some time to have her ready to explore the coast. So on the Wednesday sixteen men prepared for a land expedition. Miles Standish took command, with William Bradford, Stephen Hopkins and Edward Tilley as advisers. Hopkins, a Gloucestershire man, had been among those wrecked on Bermuda with Admiral Somers, and had gone on to Virginia. He was the only Pilgrim to have been in America before and much use was made of his experience. All the men wore armour, and carried sword and musket. They were out for three days and two nights, in the course of which they saw Indians from a distance, found a fresh-water spring where they 'drunk our first New England water with as much delight as ever we drunk drink in all our lives', found some Indian fields and buried corn, and a ship's kettle and a ruined fort that bespoke previous Europeans. William Bradford put his foot by accident into a noose of an Indian deer trap, and was swung by a bent sapling to hang head down in the air.

By 28 November, with the shallop repaired, they set out again, with thirty-four men divided between this craft and the longboat and with Christopher Jones in command. They reached further down the Cape and explored the mouth of the Pamet River which they had seen from Corn Hill, but it was too shallow to be of any use. In the bitter weather they christened it Cold Harbour, and after further explorations, in which they examined an Indian village and tried out some abandoned Indian canoes, they picked up the corn they had previously found and carried it back to *Mayflower*. While they planned their next trip the first child to be born to them in the New World arrived, to a family from Sturton-le-Steeple, William and Susanna White. They already had one son with them, called Resolved. (He was 4 years old; what had they resolved in 1616?). The second boy, whom they christened Peregrine, was to live until 1704.

Coppin, the second mate who had been on the coast before, told of a 'great navigable river and a good harbour in the other headland of this bay'. So, on Wednesday 6 December, another party was sent out. Governor Carver himself went, as well as Standish, Bradford, Hopkins, both mates of the ship, the gunner, some seamen and servants. They could hardly claw their way out of Provincetown Harbour. The salt water froze on their clothes and made them like iron, and in no time Edward Tilley and the gunner were nearly dead of cold and seasickness. But once out and in the lee of the Cape they made good progress, cleared Cold Harbour and the wide sweep of Wellfleet Harbour, and landed on the beach at dusk near the modern North Eastham. There were some Indians in the distance catching and cutting up 'a great fish like a grampus'. So they built a stockade for defence, and to keep the wind off, and slept in its lee round a fire.

Next day the shallop cruised along the long flat sandy shore while a party marched along the beach, reaching inland at likely spots but finding little more than an Indian graveyard. At nightfall they beached the shallop, built another stockade, lit their fire, mounted the usual sentries, and slept. 'About midnight we heard a great and hideous cry and our Sentinell called, Arme Arme.' After one or two musket shots from the stockade the noise ceased, and the rest of the night passed quietly. But at five in the morning, after prayers, some men were carrying things down to the boat while breakfast was being prepared, when the Indians attacked, with the same cry that they had heard in the night. Arrows flew, the men outside the stockade ran for the muskets they had put down by the shallop, and two men in the stockade opened fire while two more loaded for them. It was touch and go, but the Indians were driven off and none of the Pilgrim party injured. They picked up eighteen arrows as souvenirs, finding some of them sticking in clothing hung up on the stockade. They named the place First Encounter.

So they coasted westward along the base of the bay, seeing no likely harbour, passing the present Barnstable and the end of Cape Cod Canal. The wind freshened, with snow and rain in it, and they were glad of Coppin's assurance that there was a good harbour they could reach before nightfall. As they turned north, with wind and sea getting up (it sounds like an easterly, still the most uncomfortable blow on that coast), their rudder carried away somewhere under Manomet Heights. It was all two men could do to steer the shallop with an oar apiece over either quarter.

But ahead Coppin could see the harbour and they held on without reducing sail. Coppin mistook the apparent gaps between Gurnet Point and Saquish Island for the harbour entrance. His course took them right over Browns Bank and in the tumbling seas over its shallows the press of sail carried away the mast, broken in three parts. The men leapt to the oars and they held on to the north, only to find in the dusk and the rain the vicious line of breakers on Saquish Neck dead ahead of them. No wonder that Coppin thought this was the wrong harbour. His first reaction, and that of Clark the first mate, was to try and beach the shallop through the breakers, but an unnamed seaman at the steering oar brought the boat hard round to port, shouted to the oarsmen to row hard, and with the flood tide under them ran before the wind and seas into the quieter waters under Saquish Head. In the murk they found another island and a sheltered anchorage.

They did not know it was an island, that night. Some argued against going ashore, for fear of Indians, others were so cold and wet they would face anything rather than a night in an open boat. So they got ashore, lit a fire, and the rest were glad to join them after midnight when the wind turned north-west and put them on a lee shore. Wet through, in a hard frost and quite ignorant of what lay around them, still conscious of the arrows of that dawn, they got what sleep they could on the first night in the harbour of the new Plymouth. Sunday dawned bright and sunny; they found they were safe on an island and able to dry out. Being a Sabbath they gave thanks to God for their deliverance, dried

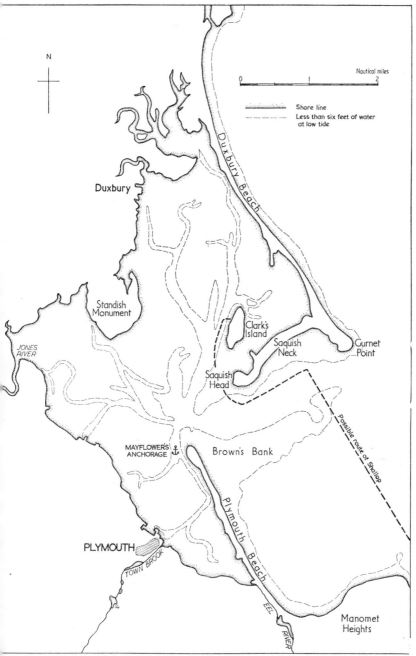

Sketch-map of Plymouth Harbour, based on modern charts. The broken line marks the possible course of the shallop on Saturday 9 December 1620, when the Pilgrims were nearly wrecked on their first entry

out their guns ('Trust the Lord, and keep your powder dry'), and rested.

The rock which sheltered them is still known as Pulpit Rock and on its sheer southern face is still carved a quotation from Winslow's account of this adventure. 'On the Sabbath Day we rested'. The island is still called Clark's Island, after the *Mayflower*'s first mate, who is reputed to have been the first man ashore.

On Monday 11 December they :

> sounded ye harbor, and founde it fitt for shipping; and marched into ye land, and found diverse cornfeilds and little running brooks, a place (as they supposed) fitt for situation; at least it was ye best they could find, and ye season, & their present necessitie, made they glad to accepte of it.

So they sailed back to the *Mayflower* with their glad news.

It was not a happy return for William Bradford for while they had been away his wife had been drowned. He had married her in Holland, whence her family had fled from Wisbech in Cambridgeshire, and though others had brought their children with them the Bradfords had left their 5 year-old John in Leyden. Dorothy was only 23 when she died; no wonder William Bradford, 7 years her elder, was to write in later years so doleful an account of Cape Cod. Before *Mayflower* weighed from Provincetown on 15 December three others had died. Scurvy, that curse of long voyages before anti-scorbutics were understood, was taking its toll.

THE CHOICE OF PLYMOUTH

A head wind gave the Pilgrims one last night at sea in *Mayflower*. Not till Saturday 16 December did the ship anchor at Plymouth. Shallow water was a problem as at Provincetown; *Mayflower* had to anchor under the limited shelter of the tip of Plymouth Beach. But once again the Sabbath was observed, with infinite patience, and not until Monday did serious exploration begin. Some parties went ashore and explored by land, and Captain Jones went off in the shallop and penetrated three miles up the river which still bears his name. After two days the choice of site was narrowed to three places. There was Clark's Island, which some favoured because it was safe against Indians (many early settlers, like the fishermen in Maine, used islands because they could more easily be defended against Indians) but there was not enough good soil or fresh water there for a permanent settlement. The Jones River site of the modern Kingston was also attractive, but it was a long way up from the fishing with which the Pilgrims hoped to make the money to pay their debts in England. That left the site of modern Plymouth.

Its first attraction was that Indians had cleared the land on both sides of what is now Town Brook, and the forest was pushed well back. It had been under cultivation, but had clearly been abandoned for several years. The brook itself made a boat-harbour and, with the springs coming out of the northern bank, gave ample fresh water. The water coming down the brook scoured the sand on either side of the mouth so that a boat could run in pretty close to the beach at all tides, and a big granite boulder, dropped by the ice cap centuries before, enabled the lively to leap ashore dry-shod and would make the basis of a simple wooden jetty. It could also be defended, and one can see the eye of Standish, the professional soldier, in the location of Leyden Street today, on the site of the original settlement. The Town Brook covers it on the south side, Cole's Hill on the north side, and Burial Hill at the back on the landward side. It was also high enough to give a good all-round view, out to sea as well as over the neighbouring forest, and was the obvious site for the small cannon the Pilgrims had brought with them.

The decision was made on the Wednesday; then for two days a storm prevented the party ashore doing anything. *Mayflower* had three anchors down for safety; the shallop made the mile and a half ashore with provisions but could not get back. In all this Isaac Allerton's wife gave birth to a still-born son. The parties who did struggle ashore to start felling timber gave constant alarms of Indians; none were seen, but muskets were never far from hand. Work had to be done when the weather permitted. Christmas Day was not a feast observed in their code: 'we went on shore, some to fell timber, some to saw, some to rive, and some to carry, so no man rested all that day.' Twenty men stayed ashore on guard; those who returned aboard were given some beer by Jones, who had spent the day refilling his fresh-water barrels.

On Thursday preparations were made for the gun platform on Burial Hill, and the little town was plotted on the ground. By persuading the single men to link themselves with a family the number of houses was kept down to nineteen. The size of the plots varied according to the number of people in the unit, but it was limited so that a stockade could be built round the whole. Indian fires and other signs that they were not far off kept everybody on their toes; the fact that the Indians themselves were never seen added to the unease. Standish took an armed party off into the forest on 4 January, but only found a few empty houses.

A common house 20 ft square was built first, and by 9 January, when it only wanted thatching, a start was made on the other houses. The sites were decided by drawing lots, and each family was to build its own 'thinking by that course men would make more haste than working in common'.

Already sickness was beginning to hit the planters, struggling against the cold and rain to build their houses, already weakened by a long spell aboard ship with no fresh fruit or vegetables to keep scurvy away. Christopher Martin was taken ill on 6 January, and five days later William Bradford collapsed as he worked. On 12 January two men cutting thatch walked off into the woods at lunchtime 'their meat in their hands'. Two dogs with them chased a deer; the men ran in pursuit and were lost. They were out all night in the frost and snow, and when they did get back at night-fall the next day, one had to have the shoes cut off his swollen feet. It was a long time before he could walk again, and he did not survive the winter. They were lodged in the common house that night, already like a hospital with as many beds as could be packed in. John Carver and William Bradford were among the sick, and they were nearly killed the next morning when a spark blew up and caught the thatched roof alight. The gunpowder was stored in the common house and each man had his loaded musket beside him; they were lucky to get out alive.

Weather only permitted three days work the next week but on 21 January the Pilgrims had their first Sunday service ashore. Prob-ably the bulk of the first rude shelters were finished and inhabited;

crude and cold they may have been but they were healthier than the typhus-ridden atmosphere that any ship developed after too long an occupation in those days. Getting the people ashore was the normal practice of the day, but fresh air was not to save many.

Six had died before the end of December; another eight were gone by the end of January, including Martin and Captain Standish's wife. In February seventeen died, including William White from Sturton-le-Steeple, and Mary Allerton, who had lost her baby at Christmas time. March took another thirteen, including Edward Winslow's wife. Whole families were wiped out. All the Mullins family went, save only 18 year-old Priscilla. Mary Chilton was left an orphan at 15. Both Tilleys and their wives died. William White was followed by his two servants, leaving his wife with two children under 5, one of whom was the baby born at Cape Cod. 'Of a hundred persons scarce fifty remain, the living scarce able to bury the dead.'

Things were no better in *Mayflower*. She lost half her ship's company, including the boatswain, the gunner, three quarter-masters and the cook. Though the seamen had at first refused to let beer be sent ashore to the sick, (it was falsely esteemed as an anti-scorbutic, and Bradford himself had cried out in his delirium 'desiring but a small cann of beere'), they found themselves so carefully tended by the Pilgrims who remained in the vessel, when their own shipmates refused to help, that they repented and sent beer ashore.

Only six or seven of the Pilgrims kept on their feet, William Brewster (who was over 50) and Miles Standish among them. They fetched wood, made fires, cooked, made the beds, washed the clothes and the bodies of their sick comrades—not the pleasantest of tasks with dysentry rife. The Indians were getting bolder, and odd ones were seen from the stricken village. The dead were buried by night on Cole's Hill, close to the houses but as far as the few fit ones could carry them, and given no grave-stones so that the Indians should not know how the ranks were being depleted. After the Indians in mid-February had stolen some tools left by a working party in the woods, a general meeting was held on the gun platform on Burial Hill at which Miles Standish was elected the military leader. While they were talking two Indians showed themselves on the hilltop to the south of Town Brook, about a quarter of a mile away, but when Standish and Hopkins went over to them they ran off. Within four days Christopher Jones, and such of his seamen as were fit, rigged lifting gear and brought the small Pilgrim cannon—two minions; a saker and two bases—up to the gun platform and helped set them up.

AN INDIAN TREATY

March brought better weather, though the toll of deaths went on. The first real contact with the Indians was established. The men were in the village discussing their military plans when a tall straight Indian with black hair hanging down his back, naked but for a leather girdle with a short fringe and armed with bow and arrows, walked boldly through the double line of houses towards the company. When stopped he greeted them in broken English, bidding them welcome. He was called Samoset, a chief from a tribe settled in Maine, and had learnt his English from the fishermen who summered on Monhegan Island. He could relate the names of several of their captains, and asked for some beer. There was none, but they gave him biscuits, butter, cheese, pudding, and part of a mallard to eat (a clue to the food of that first winter) and brandy to drink. As the wind got up they put a coat about him.

He told them that the place where they were settled was called Patuxet, and four years earlier all the Indians had been wiped out by the epidemic that had ravaged the coast. All afternoon they talked, and as night fell he showed no sign of going. Not wanting him in the village at night they suggested he went out to *Mayflower* and he agreed, but as the shallop could not get off in the high wind he was lodged in the house of Stephen Hopkins in the middle of the village, where he was well watched.

Samoset told them he had come from the tribe of Massasoit, their nearest neighbour. On the Cape were the Nausets, and he knew all about their attack on the party at First Encounter. He said their enmity to the white man dated back to Hunt's slavery raid of a few years earlier, when some of their tribe had been taken as well as the Patuxet men. Only the year before they had killed three of Dermer's men, and Dermer had been killed on Martha's Vineyard.

Samoset was sent off on the Saturday with presents of a knife, a bracelet and a ring. On the Sunday he was back with five other Indians, tall men with complexions like the gypsies in England, wearing leather chaps and aprons, with feathers in their long black hair and paint on their faces. They left their bows and arrows a quarter of a mile away and came in with furs on their arms. The English gave them food, the Indians replied with song and dance. The Pilgrims refused to trade for the furs they had brought (it was Sunday), but asked them to bring more. One sign of honesty: the Indians brought back the English tools that had been stolen in the woods.

The five went off that afternoon, but Samoset stayed until the following Wednesday. Then, with a hat, shoes, stockings, a shirt and a piece of cloth to tie about his waist (no doubt to save the English modesty), he went off. That day some more Indians appeared on the hill to the south but again made off when Standish went over to them. It was 21 March, and the last settlers were brought ashore from *Mayflower*. Most of the stores had been taken out of her at the end of January and, thus lightened, she had not been too comfortable at her anchorage.

The next day, with everyone together on shore, a business meeting was being held in the warm sunshine when Samoset came again with another four men. One was Squanto, the only survivor of the Patuxet tribe, whom Captain Dermer had brought back after his long sojourn in England only the year before. He was a pledge of English friendship and kindness. They brought some skins and fish, and the news that the Indian chief, Massasoit, was nearby with his brother and all his men. Soon the Indians appeared on the hilltop across Town Brook in full view of the English and the two parties watched each other, keeping apart. Squanto went to and fro between them as intermediary, and then Edward Winslow was sent to the Indians, bearing presents of knives and jewels for the two chiefs, a bottle of brandy, some biscuits and butter.

Winslow, aged 25, was acting as ambassador for the first time; it was a role he was often to fill later. On behalf of King James he offered friendship and peace, and explained that their governor

Plimoth Plantation; a modern reconstruction of the first village

wished to see the chief, to trade with him and live in peace as neighbours. The chief listened to Squanto's interpretation, ate and drank of the gifts and passed the rest to his men, fingered Winslow's armour and sword and offered to buy it. Then Winslow stayed with the chief's brother while Massasoit with some twenty men went down to the village, leaving their weapons behind. Miles Standish and half a dozen men armed with muskets met them at the brook, salutes were exchanged, and Massasoit was conducted to a half-finished house where a green rug and some cushions had been placed on the floor. To them the governor, John Carver, came in procession with drummer and trumpeter, and more musketeers. Carver kissed the Indian's hand, and the Indian kissed him; an interesting encounter for Massasoit's head and face shone with oil, his face was painted red, and a chain of white bone beads hung round his neck. Carver produced some brandy, drank to Massasoit, and passed him the mug. The Indian 'drunke a great draught that made him sweat all the while after.'

Then they agreed peace terms. The Indians would do the settlers no injury and, if one did, the Indians would send him in for punishment. If the Indians took anything away from the settlers Massasoit would see it restored, and the settlers would do likewise. If either his tribe, or the settlers, were attacked, they would aid each other, and he would notify all the other tribes of this compact. When either side visited the other, they would leave their arms behind. 'They made a peace with him,' wrote William Bradford later, 'which hath now continued this 24 years.'

Then Massasoit produced his tobacco and the first pipe of peace was smoked (Bradford in his History says they 'drank' tobacco). The chief admired the white men's trumpet and some of his men tried to blow it. He and his people spent the night half a mile away, and though the Pilgrims kept good watch there was no cause for alarm. Next day more visits were exchanged, presents made on both sides, and Squanto came back with a large catch of eels. Massasoit and his tribe returned to their home but Squanto, whose home the Pilgrims were after all now occupying, stayed with them. He was of the utmost value, showing them where to plant their corn, and how to catch herrings in the Town Brook to use as manure. He became their interpreter, their guide to the country around, their pilot, and an invaluable friend. In fact the peace that Massasoit gave them, and the guidance of Squanto, made the development of the colony possible. Squanto was to stay with them until he died.

MAYFLOWER SAILS AWAY

Already the Pilgrims felt secure. The weather was improving, the sickness abating, though it was not entirely gone and there were still deaths. The seamen too were recovering, and Captain Jones began to prepare for his return to England. It is a sign of the new confidence in the colony that not one of the settlers sought a passage home. When *Mayflower* sailed on 5 April she had no passengers. She was grossly under-manned but to lose half of one's crew was not uncommon in those days, though the New England voyage was generally reckoned a healthy one. Neither did she carry any cargo, to the great disappointment of Weston when she berthed in the Thames a month later.

Mayflower disappears from the story. After a refit she sailed for La Rochelle, back on her old routes, and on 19 October she was discharging Bay salt in London. On 5 March 1622 Christopher Jones was buried in the churchyard at Rotherhithe; he had been back from New England less than a year. Whether he too had been ill in that bad winter at new Plymouth is not recorded, but one suspects that the trials of the voyage had told upon him. It seems to have been the end of *Mayflower* too, for in 1624 she was described as being *in ruinis*.

There was an application to the High Court of Admiralty in May that year on behalf of Christopher Child, John Moore and the widow of Christopher Jones, owners of three-quarters of the *Mayflower*, for an appreciation of the ship's value. The purpose of this legal action, and the identity of the fourth owner, has never come to light, but it is thought that *Mayflower* never sailed again after the death of her master, and by 1624 was a rotting hulk at Rotherhithe. She was valued at £128 8s 4d ($306) by two mariners and two shipwrights of Rotherhithe, and probably she was broken up soon afterwards. Child and Moore seem to have built a new *Mayflower*, which was in London loading for New England that spring; the legal action may well have spelt the ending of the old partnership and the start of a new, with a new ship.

There is a belief that the old barn of the Quaker settlement at Jordans, near Chalfont St Giles in Buckinghamshire, was built from the timbers of the *Mayflower*. Dr Rendell Harris, a Plymouth scholar of some repute, heard this legend and produced a small book in 1920, at the time of the tercentenary celebrations of the *Mayflower* voyage, in which he proved to his own satisfaction that this was true. A great controversy raged in the literary papers for some years, but most naval historians (which Rendell Harris was not) would agree was that the barn was undoubtedly built out of the timbers of a ship the size of the *Mayflower*, by shipwrights from the Thames, but that there was no proven link with the *Mayflower*. Modern historians have even more reservations about the barn, but in its neighbourhood the story is fully accepted.

Another legend is that in the old Independent Chapel at Abingdon, on the Thames just below Oxford, the two pillars were the masts of the *Mayflower*. Dr Horrocks, who had disputed the Jordans Barn case in the *Mariner's Mirror* for 1922, also examined this story. He found three legends in fact, the others being that these pillars were the masts of the *Brielle*, which brought William of Orange to England in 1680, or that they were the masts of the *John Williams*, a missionary ship. He concluded that the pillars may have been from the *Brielle* (the chapel was built twenty years after William of Orange arrived) but could not be from the *Mayflower*.

So one may look at the barn at Jordans and wonder; if the timbers are not those of the *Mayflower* they are very like those which took the Pilgrim Fathers to the New World. The ship has disappeared but the colony flourished, and has left its mark on the history of the world.

CHAPTER FIVE

The Hungry Years

WITH THE SAILING of the *Mayflower* the depleted colony, barely fifty strong, set about their struggle for survival. Under Squanto's direction they began their first seed-time, planting some of their English wheat and pease, and the maize they had found in the abandoned Indian villages on Cape Cod. It was hard work for men and women who still were on short rations, deprived of fresh vegetables and fruit, still weak from their long winter of sickness. The weather was better, but even that could be a trial.

About the middle of the month John Carver, the governor, came out of the fields on a hot day complaining of his head. He lay down, within a few hours was unconscious, and within a few days dead. He was 54. His wife, a White from Sturton-le-Steeple and John Robinson's sister-in-law, died of a broken heart within a few weeks.

The dispirited settlers elected William Bradford in his place. He had been desperately sick that winter and was still not fully recovered, but he was one of the original Pilgrims, virtually brought up in Brewster's household at Scrooby, and a survivor of all their trials. Because of his weakness he was given a deputy to assist him, Isaac Allerton. He too had come from Leyden, where he had probably joined the community from the church at Amsterdam. These two, with Miles Standish and Edward Winslow, were to lead the colony through its formative years. Bradford was 31, Allerton 34, Standish 36 and Winslow 25. The younger generation was taking over, and though they still had the benefit of Elder Brewster's advice he was from now on the elder statesman, the religious teacher and not the civic leader.

On 12 May the first wedding took place. Edward Winslow, though only six weeks a widower, married Susanna White, a sister

Page 89 A cut-out drawing showing how stores and passengers were packed into *Mayflower*. The long-boat is stowed on the upper deck but the shallop, carried on the main deck below this, is not shown. The master is taking a sunsight on the poop; the officer of the watch is calling a steering order to the quartermaster at the whipstaff, and men are manning the windlass which hoists the yards. A seaman is cooking in the forecastle, and others are getting a cask from the hold. In this drawing are seventy-odd figures; *Mayflower* must have carried about 120 passengers and crew

Page 90 Cape Cod: (*top*) Provincetown Harbour where *Mayflower* first anchored in America. The length of the pier shows how shallow the water is; (*above*) the reproduction of the shallop off the sandy coast; (*below*) First Encounter, where exploring Pilgrims beat off an Indian attack

of Samuel Fuller, the colony's doctor. She had two small children, with Peregrine only a few months old, and the winter sickness had taken both the White family's two servants and then her husband. It was probably a marriage of survival for both of them, and as the community did not recognise marriage as a sacrament the ceremony was a civil one, performed before Bradford as a magistrate, according to the Dutch custom.

The planting done, the settlers could look about them. On 10 June, Winslow and Hopkins, with Squanto as guide, set off to find Massasoit's main village. On the way they obliged one Indian village which fed them by shooting eighty crows which were raiding the native crops, and spent the night at the modern Raynham, where the Indians had a weir to trap bass in the river. Eventually they found Massasoit at what is now Barrington, Rhode Island. Though he received them with friendship, and was pleased with their gift of a red, lace-trimmed horseman's coat from England, and had them sleep at the foot of the flea-ridden bed which he occupied with his wife, he had little food to offer them. All the way there and back they found abandoned fields and signs of the great mortality that had overtaken the Indians; thousands had died and in places the skulls and bones still lay upon the ground for there had been no one to bury them.

Soon after their return a party of ten men went off in the shallop to fetch a boy, John Billington, who had wandered off into the woods and been lost. (His brother had already nearly blown up *Mayflower* at Provincetown by making fireworks near the powder barrels.) The Indians had found him and passed him from tribe to tribe; Massasoit sent word that he was near Corn Hill on Cape Cod. The early explorers had taken their corn seed there and on this visit they recompensed the Indians for having done so. In August Squanto was out with another Indian, Hobamock, who had attached himself to them. Hobamock came back in a panic declaring that they had been attacked in an Indian village some fifteen miles away, and Squanto murdered. An armed party was sent out under Standish but Squanto was found fit and well, and brought home. Three Indians who had been wounded when Standish and his men stormed into the village were brought to Plymouth and nursed back to health. Already Plymouth was developing its Indian policy, of being fair but firm, and on both counts impressed her neighbours.

The third expedition of that first summer was northwards, to the Massachusetts tribe. They lived around what is now Boston Harbour, but to the Pilgrims that area was Massachusetts. The party of ten sailed on 18 September, with Squanto as guide, naming the prominent points on the coast as they went. At the entrance to Boston harbour the headland is still called Point Allerton, the islands are still named the Brewsters, and the place where they landed is still Squantum. Clearly this was a superior site to their own; they wished they had settled there, but were now too far committed to Plymouth to face another upheaval. At Squantum they were much impressed by the beaver coats the Indian squaws were wearing. Squanto suggested just stripping the women at musket point (presumably the men were away) but the Pilgrims would have none of this. They offered trinkets as barter, and to their embarrassment the women at once stripped off their coats and, naked, took the few beads in exchange. They did tie branches about themselves and Winslow wrote that they were more modest than some of the English women. In spite of their red faces the white men went home with a rich haul of beaver skins.

Now it was harvest time. Summer had afforded ample food; there had been plenty of cod and bass about for the catching, the occasional deer to shoot, and the ration from their original stores of a peck of meal, that is about ten pounds of oatmeal or the like, a week. With the onset of autumn there were flights of wild duck, and a large number of wild turkeys came in to supplement their table. The yield from their English seed was poor, but the Indian corn grown under Squanto's directions had done well and they could now add a peck of maize a week to their diet. The wild grapes yielded a sweet strong wine. Eleven good houses had been finished, and health had been restored with the summer weather. Massasoit came in with ninety men and for three days Pilgrims and Indians feasted together, the first Thanksgiving in the New World.

Then on 10 November came the little ship *Fortune*, from England, no bigger than the *Speedwell*. The adventurers had dispatched her within a month of *Mayflower*'s arrival back in London, and aboard her were thirty-five passengers. There was Cushman and his 14 year-old son Thomas; Jonathan, the 27 year-old son of Brewster; and John Winslow, who came to join his brothers Edward and Gilbert. Of the thirty-five passengers a dozen were from Leyden and the rest recruited by the adventurers in England; the majority of these came from London or Southwark. One, Martha Ford, whose husband had died on the voyage over, gave birth to a son on her very first night ashore.

But, family reunions over, the pleasure of seeing new faces and reinforcements past, the *Fortune* was a disappointment. One cardinal rule that had been learnt in the early seventeenth century was that, to establish a plantation, brave hearts were not enough. There had to be a regular flow of supporting stores for several years. Here was a ship, sent out promptly enough, but with more mouths to feed and not even any stores for them, let alone for the settlers of the year before. Instead Weston sent a letter complaining that *Mayflower* had been so long delayed, and had sailed home empty. A charter had been obtained (in the name of John Pierce again) from the Plymouth Company, making their settlement legal. Cushman, a deacon of the Leyden church, pleaded with the Pilgrims to sign the agreement with Weston which they had rejected at Southampton. Reluctantly they did so. The *Fortune* was laden with beaver skins and cedar clapboard, worth in all about £500 (nearly $1,200), and was dispatched within a fortnight. Cushman went back with her, as the colony's agent, leaving his son behind.

The Pilgrims had turned the other cheek. Weston's complaints had been met by an acceptance of his demands, a quick turn-round for the ship, and a valuable cargo. No doubt in return they hoped this would finance another ship in the following spring with the supplies Cushman could explain they needed. Already their clothes were in rags, and the slopchest of the *Fortune* had been cleaned out by the settlers. But the *Fortune* belied her name; a French privateer picked her up in the approaches to the Channel and took her to the Biscay coast, stripping out her cargo, robbing and half-starving Cushman and the ship's company, even taking some of the ship's gear before letting her go.

The people in Plymouth were not aware of this, but they had enough problems of their own. After the *Fortune* sailed and the newcomers, mostly young men, had been settled in with the existing families, Bradford and Allerton took stock. The Thanksgiving visit of so many Indians and the unexpected arrival of thirty-five more mouths had sharply altered the food situation. By putting everyone on half rations they could eke out their stores for six months, but that would be barely enough unless the fish came back.

Then there was Indian trouble. The tribe across Narraganset Bay in the present Rhode Island, old enemies of Massasoit's tribe, had heard that the ship had brought the white men neither food nor weapons. So they sent in a bundle of arrows tied in rattle-snake skin; Squanto explained it was a challenge. The settlers sent back the skin filled with bullets and gunpowder and a message that if they wanted war they could start when they liked. The chief would not even allow the white man's magic to stay in his country; he sent it back and no more was heard of any threats. But the Pilgrims took no chances; they began to enclose their little town with a palisade, pierced by three strong gates with four flankers (corner strong-points). As garrison commander Standish divided up the men; four companies each with a commander, a rendezvous in time of alarm, and an allocated rôle in defence. A fifth company was the fire brigade, in case an attack set fire to one of the thatched houses. By night the gates were locked, and a watch set.

Six days a week work went on, with Sunday alone for resting. On Christmas Day, as on the previous year, the men turned to, but the new men protested; it offended their consciences to work that day. Bradford therefore excused them. When the Pilgrims came home from the fields at midday the newcomers were out in the street playing, 'pitching ye barr, & some at stoole-ball, and such like sports'. So Bradford took away their gear and told them it was against his conscience that some should play while others worked; if they wanted to keep Christmas as a matter of devotion they should do so in their houses. He had no more trouble.

1622 : INDIAN THREATS

By March 1622 the palisades were finished, and by placing a fence between each house from the street to the enclosure each household acquired a private garden which could be cultivated for its own needs. It was time to resume trade with the Massachusetts, and the shallop was made ready. Now the Indian tribes were plotting together to capture both the settlement and the shallop when their forces were divided. Not taking it seriously, Standish took ten men, plus Hobamock and Squanto, into the shallop and set off. Scarcely had they sailed when one of Squanto's family came running in, his face bloody, to say the Indians were at hand and menacing the town. Guns were fired to recall Standish, and back he came to find the stockade manned. Hobamock would not believe the story, and his wife was sent quietly to Massasoit to spy out the land. She found all quiet, and told the chief of Plymouth's alarm. He sent back word that he would keep to his agreement and report if any danger threatened.

So off went Standish and his party again to the Massachusetts, and had good trade, but Squanto became suspect. It became clear that he was using his influence with the white men to strengthen his position with the Indians, telling them that he could dictate peace or war, and that he had the plague, which had so affected the tribes, buried under the floor of a hut, whence he could launch it to their destruction. What the Pilgrims did have buried was several barrels of gunpowder, in a way a 'magic' on which their safety rested.

There was jealousy between the two Indians living in Plymouth, but, even more serious, Massasoit now came to think that Squanto's influence was rivalling his own. Massasoit sent in an embassy demanding Squanto's death, and Bradford was in a quandary. The friendship of Massasoit was vital but Squanto, though he was becoming a nuisance, had by his guidance and advice enabled them to survive so far. While the debate among the leaders of the colony went on there came a diversion; a European boat was sighted off the harbour. The men stood to arms in case it was the French. But it was an English boat from the *Sparrow* which Weston and another adventurer had sent out to fish on the coast of Maine for their own profit. The boat brought a letter from Weston, and seven men. The letter blandly asked the Pilgrims to feed and shelter these men while they worked for Weston and his partner, felling timber to ship back and setting up a salt pan on an island in Plymouth

Harbour. Still no stores for the settlers, just word that the adventurers in London were beginning to break up and, because there were no returns from Plymouth, they were not willing to send John Robinson and the rest of the Leyden flock across. It was 'could comfort to feede their hungrie bellies', for the winter stocks were nearly exhausted and the summer not yet bringing more.

In all the commotion of this news, much of which Bradford and the other leaders kept from the bulk of the Plymouth colonists, the embassy from Massasoit departed, leaving Squanto in peace. Edward Winslow was sent off in the shallop to Damarin's Cove, one of the island bases off the Maine coast of the English fishing fleet, to try and get food. He found thirty vessels engaged there and they gave him what they could spare. It was not much to share among all the people in Plymouth but it tided them over, for when Winslow got back they were out of bread for the first time since their arrival, the wildfowl were gone, and though the coast was again swarming with fish they had not strong enough tackle or nets to catch them. The Indians were aware of Plymouth's weakness, and Massasoit seemed less friendly after the Squanto affair. So the Pilgrims felt it wise to divert some men from sowing the fields and set them to turn the gun platform on Burial Hill into a fort. It was one storey in height, built of heavy oak timbers, with a flat roof enclosed by breastworks. The little cannons were mounted on the roof, and a guard kept night and day. It was the biggest building in Plymouth, and took ten months to finish, but the ground floor also served as a church.

Two more ships arrived in June, the *Charity* and the *Swan*. Fifty or sixty men all strangers, came ashore, and letters from England. Weston had sold up his shares in the Plymouth adventure, had got a charter of his own, and had sent these men to establish it. But, as the *Charity* was first going down to Virginia with stores, would Plymouth kindly feed these men till the ship got back? A letter from Cushman warned them that the newcomers were not the kind of men for Plymouth; John Pierce wrote on the back of Cushman's letter that these men were 'not fitt for an honest mans company.'

But Plymouth took them in, and gave them shelter and food for the whole summer. They were an idle crew, offering no help either in the fields or on the fort. The Plymouth men, on half rations all winter and weak with hunger even now in the summertime, were hardly strong enough to till their fields properly and had to put up with these wretches stealing the ears as they formed on the corn. Not even whippings for those who were caught made much difference. The work in the fields was vital for survival, and news of the massacre of many of the English in Virginia gave fresh

The fort at Plimoth Plantation, a reconstruction of the main defence against Indians or raiders from the sea. Religious services were held on the ground floor, lit only by two small windows and musket slits

impetus to the fort building. One of the English captains fishing off Maine took the trouble to send a boat to Plymouth with the news. Jamestown had been growing apace; its settlers were approaching a population of 4,000 and they had spread far out, setting up estates and homesteads well away from the town. All these scattered settlers the Indians had slaughtered at Easter, killing nearly 400 people most brutally; only those who had the protection of the town had escaped.

After this unhappy summer came a poor harvest. Inadequate hoeing, and the pilfering, meant that they gathered less than enough to see them through to another harvest. It was a relief when a ship came in from Jamestown from which they could buy (with beaver skins, at exorbitant rates) the beads and knives with which to barter with the Indians, for Plymouth had even come to the end of its trading goods.

A passenger in the ship, John Pory, going home after three years as secretary to the Virginia colony, gives the first outside account of the colony in some of his letters. He wrote that John Clark, their pilot ('a more forward undertaker then performer') had meant to take them to Cape Ann, the present Gloucester, Mass, but had stumbled on Plymouth by accident. Pory underlined the good terms the Pilgrims had established with the Indians, and the richness of their land. Eels were available most of the year, alewives or herrings came up the Town Brook in April or May to spawn in the ponds in such quantities that they could be taken up in hogsheads, and those not needed for food were used for manure. There was fish all summer better than Thames salmon, lobsters so big and numerous that no man would believe, waterfowl, vines yielding better grapes than anything in Virginia, plenty of deer and large fat turkeys. They had enclosed their town with a palisade 2,700 ft around, stronger than any in Virginia, and a blockhouse where, in spite of their friendship with the Indians, a guard was manned night and day. Pory borrowed from Brewster a commentary on the first five books of the Bible to read on his voyage home, and sailed away. His convivial and scholarly conversation must have been a welcome refreshment for the elder.

It was a relief when the *Swan* came back to say that a suitable place for Weston's new colony had been found at Wessagusset, in the present town of Weymouth, Mass. It was only twenty-five miles away, and would mean competition for the Massachusetts trade, but the Plymouth people were glad to see the *Charity* also come back from Virginia to take these sixty hungry mouths away. Even then the sick were left behind for Plymouth to go on looking after.

The little *Swan* was left at Wessagusset, and now the new settlement suggested a joint expedition, using this vessel, to trade around Cape Cod. Both the *Swan* and the Plymouth shallop were sent, with

Bradford in command (Standish being sick) and Squanto as pilot. But he could not lead them through the shoals around Monomoy Island at the south of the Cape, so they went ashore at the present Chatham and obtained some corn.

There Squanto took sick and died in a few days, asking his English friends to pray that he might go to the Englishman's God in heaven. He had given the Pilgrims their first welcome to the New World, he had been their guide, interpreter and teacher, and in many ways made their survival possible. He had lived in Spain and England and if this, and his influence with the Plymouth settlers, made him feel superior to his Indian brethren it was a human failing. Squanto merits his place in New England history, and one hopes that God too could find him a corner in heaven.

Their pilot lost, the party turned back and used a fair wind to reach across to Massachusetts, where they persuaded the Indians to plant extra corn. But they found sickness among the Indians, discontent with the behaviour of the new settlement, and such a rate of barter set up by the new men that the balance of trade was quite unreasonable. So back they sailed to the bottom of Cape Cod Bay, where they found good trade. But storms cast the shallop so high up the beach that they had to bury their corn, abandon the ship, and walk the fifty miles back to Plymouth.

1623: THE FIRM HAND

Early in January 1623 Standish went down and fetched back both shallop and corn, and so Plymouth came through its second winter, ranging the coast by boat and reaching inland to buy corn where it could. In the course of their travels the Pilgrims discovered the narrowness of the base of Cape Cod peninsula, and that only a few miles of land separated Cape Cod Bay from Buzzards Bay, into which the Dutch came at times for trade. So when, in March, word came that Massasoit was very ill and that there was a Dutch ship ashore near his house, it was decided to send off Edward Winslow (who spoke Dutch) and another man, with Hobamock as guide. The Dutch ship was away before they reached there, but Massasoit was nearly dead. Although no doctor Winslow set to work and restored him to health.

In gratitude Massasoit reported a plot among the Indians, which he had refused to join, to destroy the Wessagusset settlement. Winslow would already have heard enough about the behaviour there not to be surprised. Weston's men had started out by cheating the Indians and sleeping with their women; they had wasted the supplies they had started with, given away their clothes and bedding to get more, and finally gone as servants to the Indians to earn some food. Now they were enduring every insult, and had even hanged one incurable thief to appease their new masters. Plymouth had already had to restrain them from taking what they wanted from the Indians by force of arms. Now the Indians proposed to get rid of them but, realising that Plymouth would never tolerate this, planned to destroy the older settlement as well.

So Winslow made his way back through the allegedly plotting Indian tribes, accepting their hospitality as he went and even discussing Christian ethics with one. The conversation started when the chief observed the English saying Grace before their meal; the Indians seem to have accepted Winslow's version of the Christian beliefs and agreed that it was in accord with most of their views, though they thought the seventh commandment would mean many inconveniences, tying a man to one woman.

Winslow reported the plot to Plymouth, where some inklings of the news had already arrived. The Pilgrims never lacked for courage, and Standish was sent off with eight men by boat to Wessagusset. He warned the white men there, and pretended to trade with the Indians. By enduring a few days of insult he sorted out the ringleaders and then killed the principal with his own knife. Several Indians were killed, some hanged, and the rest fled the settlement. But it was no longer tenable. Standish offered its former inhabitants sanctuary at Plymouth but they preferred to take what food he could spare and set off in the *Swan* for Maine. It was late March, nearly time for the English fishing vessels to be arriving.

Standish went back to Plymouth with the head of the Indian leader, which was promptly stuck on a pike above the now-finished fort. Its first occupant a few days earlier had been a Massachusetts Indian suspected of spying out their weaknesses. In later letters from Leyden the Rev John Robinson was to upbraid them for killing instead of converting Indians, and little fiery Standish has since been condemned for his bloody handling of the situation. But these were men holding on to life on the most remote frontier of the seventeenth century. Less than a century before old Plymouth had hoisted a Cornish head above its Guildhall; twenty years after this the Civil War in England was to show as much brutality and often for less cause. Sufficient to say that Plymouth had many years of peace with the Indians after this sharp affray, and that this one firm blow against one tribe persuaded all the others to keep their peace. They had also got rid of a rival colony whose conduct did them no good.

Oddly enough Thomas Weston, who had tried to plant the Wessagusset colony for his own profit, turned up in person the same month. He was deeply in debt in England through his various ventures, and a warrant was out for him. He had come out with the fishing fleet, under an assumed name and calling himself a blacksmith. Getting a boat and a couple of men he had set out on a private exploration of the coast but had been wrecked, plundered by Indians, and stripped to his shirt. When Weston reached Plymouth he had acquired a suit of clothes but no more. The rôles were reversed, the English merchant who had so many times denied the supplies that were necessary for their joint success now came to them a suppliant. Though their beaver skins were their only way of trading for food, and though the Pilgrims still did not trust him, yet they let him have a hundred skins which put him on his feet again on the Maine coast. These skins were Weston's salvation but he never paid the Pilgrims for them, except with slander behind their backs.

After this visit the Pilgrims changed their method of working. That spring, instead of communal planting, every household was allotted roughly an acre a head of ground on which to plant their own crops. There seems to have been rather more and better land for the *Mayflower* settlers, and rather less for the *Fortune* people, but no doubt this was fair enough. Each plot was to be taxed to feed the officers and fishermen whose duties prevented their giving so much time to the fields. But it was not a good spring, and a drought of six weeks after planting held everything back. The shallop was rigged as a fishing boat and kept at sea, the women and children dug for clams on the beach, and so another hungry season limped by. Yet faith did not desert them; a public day of fasting and prayer was appointed and the next day a gentle rain began; 'it was hard to say whether our withered Corn, or drouping affections were most quickened or revived.'

CHAPTER SIX

More Settlements

STANDISH CAME BACK from a food-buying expedition in April 1623 with a new neighbour, David Thompson. A Scot long domiciled in Plymouth, England, he had taken a large grant of land from the Plymouth Virginia Company and, financed by three merchants of the port, Nicholas Sherwell among them, had settled at the mouth of the Piscataqua in the modern Rye, New Hampshire. He was the first arrival of a new wave of settlers which came from a spurt of energy by Ferdinando Gorges. In 1622 Gorges had joined with Captain John Mason, a former governor of Newfoundland, to obtain a grant from the Council of New England, confirmed by the king, of all the land between the Merrimac, which enters the sea just north of Cape Ann, and the Kennebec. (In 1629 they divided this between them, Mason taking all the area south of the Piscataqua, which he called New Hampshire after his home in England, and Gorges all the land north of that river, which he called New Somerset after his own home. There is still a Somerset county, but the old name of Maine persisted.)

Gorges planted a settlement on Monhegan Island to support the summer fishermen, and in a year or so sold the island to a merchant of old Plymouth, Abraham Jennings, whose son graduated from Leyden University in 1628. From now on there was a steady flow of arrivals with a strong representation of men and money from old Plymouth among them; in the year that Thompson crossed the Atlantic the English port sent eighty emigrants in one ship alone. All the new establishments were small and scattered, little more than trading posts and not communities like Plymouth. But from this time forward the Pilgrims were not alone in New England.

Gorges and Mason decided that no one could fish upon the coast without their licence, and late in June the *Plantation* came into new Plymouth. Her captain, Thomas West, was the new 'Admiral of New England', but he was to find it as hard to get the sturdy characters out summer fishing on the coast to pay him any dues as his employers were to retain the vast and nearly empty lands they had awarded themselves.

The next ship that summer, the *Anne*, which was followed a fortnight later by the storm-battered *Little James*, was more welcome. They brought eighty-seven settlers for new Plymouth, of whom twenty-nine were from Leyden, the biggest reunion for three years. One was a woman of 80. There were the two Brewster daughters, Patience and Fear, Samuel Fuller's wife Bridget, and a number of wives and children who had waited in Leyden while the husbands established themselves in the New World. There had not been room for all who wished to come.

Two brides came out. One, by tradition the younger sister of Miles Standish's first wife who had died in the dreadful first winter of 1621, very quickly married her former brother-in-law. The other was Mrs Alice Southworth, widow of a Sturton-le-Steeple silk-worker. Within a few weeks she married the governor, William Bradford; probably both women had received proposals from their prospective husbands before they left England.

Many of the newcomers wondered what they had committed themselves to, for they were welcomed by a ragged enough band of planters, 'some litle beter than halfe naked', who could only offer them in welcome a lobster or a piece of fish washed down with spring water. The bread was long exhausted. But resolutely the old planters decided that they would leave the supplies that came in the two ships to the new arrivals, and that they would wait for their own harvest. After the bad crop of the previous year they were afraid that their own corn would not last out the swollen colony for the next winter if they had to share it.

But the bounty of the summer was close at hand, and when Bradford married Alice Southworth on 14 August there was a great wedding feast. Emmanuel Altham, one of the adventurers who had come out in charge of the newcomers, described it in a letter home:

> We had about twelve pasty venisons, besides others, pieces of roasted venison and other such good cheer in such quantity

that I could wish you some of our share. For here we have the best grapes that ever you saw—and the biggest, and divers sorts of plums and nuts. . . .

Five Indian chiefs came in for the wedding, including Massasoit, who tactfully only brought one of his five wives, and about 120 other Indians with their bows and arrows. The planters greeted them by firing off their muskets; the bows and arrows were put into the governor's house, and the Indian wedding presents of three or four bucks and a great turkey delivered. 'And so we had very good pastime in seeing them dance, which is in such manner, with such a noise that you would wonder.'

Clearly the Pilgrims knew how to enjoy themselves. Altham says that when they arrived they found all the plantation in good health, 'neither man, woman or child sick'. There were about twenty houses, 'four or five of which are very fair and pleasant'. In this letter of 1623, Altham always described the plantation by its Indian name of Patuxet; the following May a letter from him calls it Plymouth.

But whatever the alarms of the people who came out with him, there was no need for worry. The new plan of everyone planting for himself instead of for the commonwealth, and everyone tending his own, brought such a bumper crop that never again was Plymouth to run short of bread, and indeed from that time on there was a surplus to sell.

The *Anne* was on charter. She was loaded up with clapboard and the furs accumulated for the past year, and Edward Winslow took passage back to England in her to act as agent in buying necessities for the next ship out. The *Little James* and her crew stayed as the colony's fishing boat, not for local food but to salt and dry the catches for export to Europe. Among the newcomers were nine 'particulars' who were not to form part of the colony in the sense that they subscribed to the old agreement with the adventurers in London, but were there to trade for themselves. Areas were allocated to them where they could build houses, but they were required to submit to the general discipline of the governor, to pay their share into the common store, and not to trade with the Indians until the colony's communal agreement had run out. They were exempt from any general employment except defence.

The settlers in the New World were building up. In September a ship arrived from Plymouth with Captain Robert Gorges aboard, son of Sir Ferdinando. He had come to set up a plantation in the Bay of Massachusetts, and had chosen Wessagusset, where Weston's men had made such a disastrous start. Plymouth was told that Captain Gorges held a commission as governor general of the whole country, but that he was including Bradford, the Governor of Plymouth, in his council. While Gorges was at anchor in Plymouth harbour Weston himself turned up in a small craft, to be at once charged by Gorges with setting up a colony which had disturbed the peace, and doing various other things to the detriment of Sir Ferdinando and his company. Bradford spoke up for Weston, he was discharged, and Gorges went off to his colony. After some months of charges and counter-charges against Weston, he took himself off to Virginia and out of the Plymouth story. Without him in the first place, perhaps, the Pilgrims would never have got to Plymouth, but they might have fared better in cleaner hands. Weston eventually died of the plague in Bristol, England, during the Civil War.

Robert Gorges did not stay for the winter, and without effective leadership the second colony on Massachusetts Bay broke up. Fire destroyed some of the houses and the men drifted away, some back to England, some down to Virginia, until within a year all were gone. Nor did the *Little James* prosper. With Altham aboard she made a poor trading voyage round Cape Cod, offering the Indians goods inferior to those they could get from the Dutch at New Amsterdam, and only escaped being wrecked on Browns Bank when she got back to Plymouth in a storm by cutting away her mainmast. Next spring she went up to Maine to fish, but she was wrecked off David Thompson's settlement in New Hampshire on the way back, with the captain and two men drowned.

1624: JOHN LYDFORD AND JOHN OLDHAM

The Pilgrims never had any joy in the fish business, 'a thing fatall to this plantation', Bradford was already saying. So they

Page 107 (*above*) Plymouth Rock patterned by the shadows of visitors looking down at it; (*below*) Indian country; the 'wading place' near the modern Middleborough, Mass, on the Pilgrim route from Plymouth to Massasoit's village

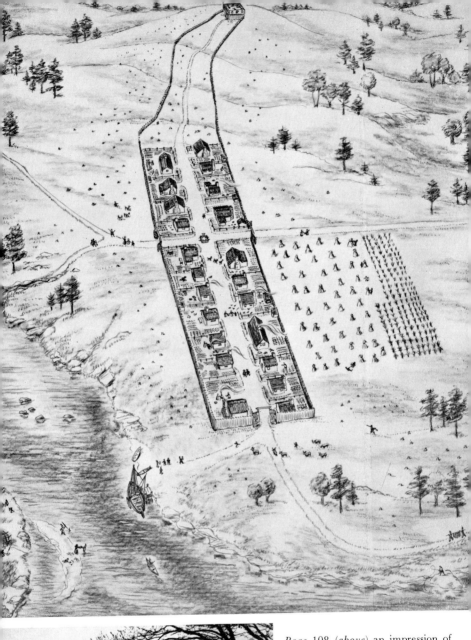

Page 108 (*above*) an impression of
the early settlement with the fort
on the hill, the shallop in Town
Brook, and a boy fishing from
Plymouth Rock; (*left*) a cove at
Stage Fort Park, Cape Ann, where
the Pilgrims had their fishing stage.
Gloucester is in the background

were not especially cheered when Edward Winslow returned in the *Charity*, with all the equipment for a fishing venture. The adventurers felt this a better investment than mere supplies for the colony. They had a patent to set up a base at Cape Ann, at the present town of Gloucester, Mass, and sent a carpenter to build the small craft which would do the actual fishing, and the platforms on the shore on which the fish would be dried. Another man came to make salt pans ashore, where by evaporating the sea-water the wherewithal could be obtained to salt fish down, an alternative to drying it. In the usual fishing pattern of Newfoundland and Maine, the *Charity* would act as mother ship and take the catch back to Europe, probably Spain or Portugal, in the autumn.

For Plymouth itself, however, Winslow had made a most valuable purchase, three heifers and a bull, the first domestic cattle in New England; Altham in 1623 had only seen goats, pigs and hens in Plymouth. Winslow also brought a supply of clothing, long overdue, and a minister, the Rev John Lydford. Ever since the original voyage the settlers from Leyden had been hoping for the comfort of having their own pastor, John Robinson, join them; but it was becoming increasingly clear that the adventurers were not particularly anxious to finance the passage of any more people from Leyden, least of all Robinson. This meant real hardship for the settlers; they had come for religious freedom and, though they had the preaching of Brewster, they had not been able to make their communion or baptise their children. In his letters Robinson made it sharply clear that the sacraments could only be administered by a properly-ordained pastor and not by a teaching elder. Some of the 'particulars' had sent home complaints of the conditions of life in Plymouth to the adventurers, including this absence of the sacraments (though one may suspect from the behaviour of some 'particulars' that they were not an especially godly crew).

But it was springtime. Last year's harvest had been so good that the new planting system was to be kept. The people had begun to use their corn as a form of money, and were anxious moreover that they could carry over the advantage of one year's manuring and careful tilling to another. It was decided that there would be no more annual balloting for plots of land; that each settler was to be given the ownership of his one acre. So Plymouth once more

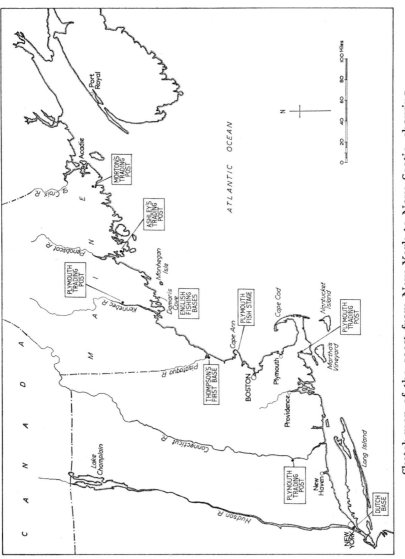

Sketch-map of the coast from New York to Nova Scotia, showing the range of the Pilgrim activities

hoed and sowed, and the *Charity* went off to Cape Ann. Her crew, however, had been recruited late in the season when the West-country boats had taken up the best men. The master was a drunk-ard, and the salt-maker an 'ignorante, foolish, self-willed fellow'. The carpenter was a good man who quickly made two good shal-lops and a strong lighter, and prepared the wood for stages (as the fish-drying platforms were known) for two catches, all of local timber, hewn from the forest, but he died of fever. Not surprisingly the *Charity* had an unprofitable summer, but the shallops she brought back to Plymouth proved very useful.

Plymouth was not too happy either. The Rev Mr Lydford, who had early offended local opinion by baptising a child with the sign of the cross, had entered into league with John Oldham, the lead-ing spirit among the 'particulars' who had arrived the year before. Being suspicious, Bradford did not scruple to intercept and read the letters they sent home in the *Charity*, and found them plotting against his government and planning to reform the Plymouth church. Oldham refused to stand his watch, and drew a knife on Standish when ordered to do so. Eventually they were both brought to trial before the whole community, accused not only of these offences but also of libelling the settlement to the adventurers in England. Both were ordered to be expelled from the colony, Oldham immediately (though his family could stay until he made provision for them), and Lydford with his family within six months.

Lydford, who had used an ingratiating manner to win favour when he first arrived, soon wormed his way back into their con-fidence. Once there he began his old tricks, and his letter writing. The *Little James* had been salvaged and was to be sent back to England; once again a Lydford letter was found aboard. So, his time expired, he was brought up for censure again and now even his wife gave evidence against him, exposing him as a lecherous hypocrite with a long record of trouble over women and illegiti-mate children.

1625: THE LITTLE JAMES

Oldham now came back as bold as brass to start trouble and he was forced to run the gauntlet through a line of men, each of whom 'gave him a thump on ye brich, with ye but end of his musket' and out of the colony.

This was the spring of 1625. Jack Oldham was actually running the gauntlet when vessels from England arrived with Winslow back from his second winter in England. Winslow had had trouble with Lydford's friends in London, and the adventurers' company was fast breaking up. A letter he brought declared that the adventurers had spent £1,400 ($3,300) in settling the colony and required the planters to send back what they could to be sold until this debt was paid off. The goods the company sent over: cattle, a few horses (the first), clothing, stockings, shoes, and so forth, were not supplies as before but goods to be sold to the planters. Winslow and Allerton were the appointed agents of the company but they were required to charge forty per cent on these goods for carriage. The skins and boards sent back as payment were to be debited thirty per cent for carriage, so the people of Plymouth reckoned that they were paying seventy per cent over price for what they received. Yet they had no choice, no other market.

Two ships had come over, the *White Angel* and the salvaged *Little James*, which had been seized by one of the adventurers for debt and was fishing for him privately. They went off to Cape Ann for the season, only to find that the friends of Oldham and Lydford had taken over the Plymouth fishing stage. Altham says that Plymouth sent armed men to regain their stage and that the newcomers at once yielded it up. As it happened the rival boat had a poor season and this group never ventured again. Lydford and Oldham were heard of variously on the coast, Lydford eventually dying in Virginia and Oldham being murdered by Indians.

But the Plymouth ships had a good season, and sailed in the autumn well laden with fish and furs. The *White Angel* towed *Little James* across the Atlantic, but because of war with Spain (it was the year Charles II came to the throne and that autumn he had launched the calamitous attack upon Cadiz) she could not use the profitable Peninsular markets but had to make for England. Just off old Plymouth she cast off the tow of the *Little James* and almost at once the small ship was seized by a Sallee rover, one of the North African pirates which had been terrorising the English Channel since the Stuart kings let the navy sink into impotence.

The *Little James* was carried off, deeply laden with salt, cod and £800 (over $1,800) worth of beaver skins, into Barbary. Miles Standish had a lucky escape, for he had gone to England this time as the colony's agent and had intended taking passage in the *Little James*. But he sailed in the big ship and so escaped the slavery into which the captain and crew of the *Little James* were cast. But Standish had trouble enough; Parliament and King Charles were at loggerheads and the country full of plague which the army had brought back from Spain. With the loss of one cargo and the collapse of the market for the other, the adventurers were in no shape to finance another venture. Standish managed to borrow £150 ($360) at fifty per cent and, though much went on his expenses, he bought what supplies the colonists needed and found a fishing vessel bound for Maine to take him and his goods back.

1626: ROBINSON'S DEATH

The Plymouth men had now turned sailors. A good harvest had given them a surplus of corn, so they decked one of the shallops made for them the year before at Cape Ann, sent her up to the Kennebec River in Maine with Winslow as master, and she brought home £700 ($1,670) worth of beaver skins and some other furs. In spring 1626, when word came that Standish was in Maine, they sent the shallop again to fetch him and his goods home.

He brought sad news for the Pilgrims from Leyden, particularly for the few who had left Scrooby with them twenty years before. John Robinson their pastor was dead. His brother-in-law Roger White sent off a letter soon after his death on 1 March 1625 but it was the following spring before Standish could deliver it. For the leaders like Bradford and Brewster especially this was a blow, for Robinson had not only been their minister but their philosopher, the director of their thought. He had shaped and fashioned the ideas which had led them to endure oppression in England, the perils of their escape and poverty in Holland. What was more, he had shared it with them. Though they knew there were adventurers who opposed his going to the New World, and that there was no hope of getting them to finance his crossing, there was always the hope that one good fishing season, one good cargo of beaver skins, might bring him over to them. Now death had carried him off; he was not quite 50. For all the Leyden people, still the core and heart of the Plymouth settlement, it was a bitter blow.

It was indeed a letter full of death, for it told the Pilgrims that Robert Cushman, who had worked so hard for the colony, was also dead. King James, who had been the cause of their leaving the Church of England, and Prince Maurice of Orange who by forcing a truce with the Spaniards had made Holland a refuge for them, had also died in the same year; the Pilgrims had much to ponder upon.

There was also work to do. The corn was planted. Lacking goods for trading with the Indians, and hearing that the plantation at Monhegan Island was breaking up, Bradford and Winslow went off by boat with a few men to see what they could buy. David Thompson joined them and between them they bought all there was to be had, including some goats and a supply of corn. A French ship had also been wrecked there and the fishing fraternity had the cargo from her, which Plymouth also bought up. The total cost was £500 ($1,190) paid partly in beaver skins and partly on a bill of credit from a Bristol merchant. A good summer's trading and a good harvest enabled them to clear this bill, the money Standish had borrowed, and some other debts. In the autumn Isaac Allerton was sent off to England to settle up, to come to terms with the adventurers, and to take up more credit to finance their trading. With more white settlers on the coast the Indians were putting their prices up and a bigger boat was needed to make these expeditions pay. So a house carpenter among them, who had worked with the shipwright at Cape Cod, cut one of his shallops in half, lengthened it by five or six feet, decked it, and rigged it ready for service the next spring. It was to serve them well for the next seven years.

That winter a small ketch, the *Sparrowhawk*, bound for Virginia with twenty-five passengers and goods, was cast ashore on the south-west side of Cape Cod, at the modern Orleans. Hearing this from the Indians, Bradford took salvage gear across the bay and ported it over the narrow isthmus (it was no weather to go round the Cape). He gave the survivors food, and the gear, but had hardly returned to Plymouth when word came again that the

Sparrowhawk was a total wreck. So her company, made up of a few gentlemen with a large number of Irish servants, was brought into Plymouth. To keep the men employed, and because they could not leave for some time, they were allotted some land to prepare for the spring sowing.

1627: EXIT THE ADVENTURERS

Allerton came back in the spring of 1627 (the spring and autumn crossings of the Maine fishermen were still the only links with England). He had reached an agreement with the adventurers, who had by now invested some £7,000 ($16,700) in Plymouth, to buy them out for £1,800 (nearly $4,300) to be paid in annual sums of £200 ($476), the first instalment falling due in September 1628. It was a reasonable bargain, though it represented a tremendous strain on a colony of 32 houses and some 180 people who still had to earn their keep and finance their trading. But the agreement was signed and, though mortgaged, Plymouth was their own.

Next came the division. The governor and four or five of the principal men who had done so much for the community were given their houses free. Each other household was given its own house, but they were all valued and those above average were charged to compensate those below. The livestock was divided, one cow, two goats and several pigs to every six people. The trading was to go on as before to pay the common debts, and in this each man had one share, the married men also having the option to purchase one for each member of his household. Servants had no shares, save what their employers chose to give them. Every shareholder was allotted twenty acres of land in addition to his original acre. One can imagine that a whole series of town meetings were needed to sort out all the problems and ensure as fair a deal as possible. All the latecomers were treated on equal terms with the original settlers; only those who had put money in the original project were, in justice, better treated. They had an extra share for each £10 ($24) invested.

All this intense business was giving the colonists quite enough to think about, when Fells, a leader of the shipwrecked party bound for Virginia, was found to be sleeping with his maidservant. He

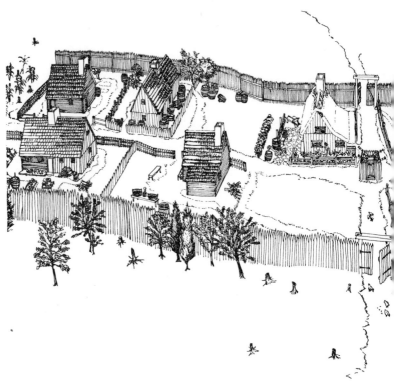

Plimoth Plantation; a drawing of

constructed settlement of 1627

and his community were packed off to Virginia at the first opportunity. That was not until the end of the summer, when these temporary residents had raised a good harvest of corn from the land given them, and paid for the food supplied by the Plymouth people from their ample stock of cloth, stockings, shoes, and the like. In spite of Fells, and some trouble with one or two others, the stay had been generally satisfactory and mutually profitable. John Sibsey, one of the party, settled near Norfolk in Virginia and became a councillor of the colony.

Over 300 years later the timbers of their ship, the *Sparrowhawk*, were found in the sand of Cape Cod, reassembled, and are now on show in Pilgrim Hall, Plymouth. Though she is only half the size of *Mayflower*, ships of her dimensions were not uncommon among the Atlantic voyagers of the seventeenth century, of which *Sparrowhawk* alone survives.

Her passengers, going south in 1627, had to pass a new colony between Plymouth and Virginia. After years of trading in the Hudson River the Dutch settled Fort Amsterdam in 1624, on Manhattan Island. (This might have been called Plymouth but for one rough winter afternoon in 1620, and so not needed its later name change to New York.) These new colonists were ranging the coast for beaver skins and in March 1627 the governor sent a polite letter to Plymouth, extending greetings and compliments, saying that one of their boats had reached within half a day's journey of their town, and suggesting that they might have some beaver or otter to sell for ready money. Plymouth sent back an equally polite letter, saying they were well supplied for the moment but there might be future opportunities if the rates the Dutch offered were reasonable.

Behind the courtesy was a fear of the Dutch reaching into their trading area. In a roadless country the sea was still the smoothest route, but Cape Cod and its shoals made a barrier to the south of Plymouth. Something had to be done to circumvent this if they were to compete with the Dutch. That summer, a party went by sea to the bottom of Cape Cod Bay, crossed the narrow neck of land to Aptuxet, in the present village of Bourne on the shores of Buzzards Bay, and there built a house and a small boat. Some of the hired men were stationed there, keeping a few pigs and growing corn, and ready to go trading in their boat when opportunity arose. The goods obtained could be carried across the narrow neck of land and then shipped on to Plymouth. Today the Cape Cod Canal does the same job, on the same line.

Similarly, to extend their trading area northwards, Allerton was again sent off to England that autumn to get a patent to set up a trading post on the Kennebec River in Maine. Their fishing venture the previous year had shown them that David Thompson, (now moved to the island which still bears his name in Massachusetts Bay), and the fishing fleets were doing good trade with the Indians, and Plymouth had no desire to be left out of this trade.

One further commission was given to Allerton. The allocation of shares and responsibilities in the now self-owning colony was all very just, but not very practicable. A new scheme was put up at a town meeting. Apart from £1,800 (nearly $4,300) owed to the adventurers other debts amounted to £600 (over $1,400). Bradford, Standish and Allerton were willing to take over all responsibility for paying these debts; in return they were to have use of the colony's boats, all the stores, and all the trade. Each shareholder was to pay the undertakers, as the new partners styled themselves, three bushels of corn or six lb of tobacco (was this an export from Virginia, or a new crop or a hope? There is no evidence that Plymouth ever grew tobacco). The undertakers each year would import £50 ($120) worth of hose and shoes, which they would sell for corn at 6s (75 cents) a bushel. The agreement was to run for six years, and this Plymouth accepted.

The undertakers were permitted to bring in partners; William Brewster, Edward Winslow, John Howland, John Alden and Thomas Prence joined them and through Allerton they appointed James Sherley, a London goldsmith, and John Beauchamp, a London salt-merchant, to act as their agents. These had been members of the old company and better disposed towards the colonists than most. They could get money at six or eight per cent in London as against the fantastic rates at which the colonists had been forced to borrow. It says much for the fur profits that they could stand such charges. The London undertakers were willing to forgo the debts due to them for a couple of years, and had persuaded a couple of their old associates to do the same. The first payment to clear the main debt to the adventurers had been paid, trade was good, the first patent for the Kennebec obtained (not altogether satisfactory), and the new London friends were joining in the hopes that next year ships could be engaged to transport the rest of the Leyden people.

1628: DUTCH VISITORS

While Allerton was about this business in London the colony had a satisfactory visit from Isaac de Rasieres, secretary of the Dutch settlement. He had come up by sea to Plymouth's trading post on Buzzards Bay and landed to a flourish of trumpets. A boat was sent to meet him on the Cape Cod Bay side and bring him to Plymouth, where he stayed for several days. He has left a splendid description of Plymouth:

> The houses are constructed of clapboards with gardens also enclosed behind and at the sides with clapboards, so that their houses and courtyards are arranged in very good order, with a stockade against sudden attack; and at the end of the streets there are three wooden gates. In the centre, on the cross street, stands the Governor's house, before which is a square stockade upon which four patereros (cannon) are mounted so as to enfilade the streets. Upon the Hill they have a large square building with a flat roof, built of thick sawn planks stayed with oak beams, upon the top of which they have six cannon, which shoot iron balls of four and five pounds, and command the surrounding countryside.
>
> The lower part they use for their church, where they preach on Sundays and the usual holidays. They assemble by beat of drum, each with his musket or firelock, in front of the captain's door; they have their cloaks on and place themselves in order, three abreast, and are led by a sergeant with beat of drum. Behind comes the Governor in a long robe; beside him, on the right hand, comes the Preacher with his cloak on, and on the left hand the Captain with his sidearms and cloak on, and with a small cane in his hand; and so they march in good order, and each sets his arms down near him. Thus they are constantly on their guard night and day.

When he returned, some of the men went with him to the trading post and bought some of the Dutch goods. For years after, this was an exchange point between Plymouth and New Amsterdam, Plymouth selling much tobacco to the Dutch in return for sugar, linens and other cloths, to their mutual advantage.

Even more important, the Dutch sold the colonists £50 ($120) of wampum. This was only strings of shells used by the Indians south of Cape Cod and made up into belts or necklets, but the Indians used it as money. It was little known north of the Cape and it was some years before Plymouth could fully push the idea. Eventually however it became the basis of trade in both Massachusetts and Maine and through it Plymouth largely gained a monopoly of the Indian trade in those areas. Not until 1652 did Massachusetts begin to mint the pine-tree shilling which was the first real currency in New England. It was valued at six to one Spanish dollar, the West Indies currency which in time became the basis of the American dollar.

The new trading post on the Kennebec was set up very carefully, well up the river at Fort Western, in the present city of Augusta. Nearly fifty miles up the river, it was well into Indian territory, and cut off the flow of skins to the fishermen on the coast. The new post was not above buying from the fishing fleet, however, and offered the Indians coats, shirts, rugs, blankets, biscuit, peas, and prunes, as well as Plymouth-grown corn. It is a far cry from the conditions of five years before when the ragged, half-starved colonists had not even a crust of bread to put with their fish and water diet. Nor were they alone on the coast. Between the new Kennebec trading post and Plymouth there were now eight small groups, 'ye straggling planters' Bradford called them. One of them now began to cause all the rest some alarm.

A Captain Wollaston with several other gentlemen and a number of servants had established themselves on the shores of Massachusetts Bay, in the modern Quincy, in 1625. After a time Wollaston went to Virginia and there he found a considerable demand for his servants. After the custom of the time they were bound to him for a number of years, and he could 'sell them', or the unexpired years of their bond, to the planters. This was so profitable that he sent to England for more servants. Here were Englishmen being bought and sold; no wonder the same thing could happen to black men without any concern. Virginia already had some negroes. But Captain Wollaston's bond men were concerned and a lawyer, Thomas Morton, led them to rebel against becoming exports. They expelled Wollaston's deputy and renamed Mount Wollaston as Merry Mount. They turned their trading profits into strong drink, took Indian women for their pleasure, set up a maypole and celebrated 'ye beasly practieses of ye madd Bacchinalians'.

Various neighbours protested and one cut down the maypole, but when Merry Mount began selling the Indians alcohol and guns, (the French in the north, and some of the fishermen, had already been doing this, to the alarm of the settlers), and taught them how to make gunpowder and cast bullets, it was really time to act. The straggling plantations, being most vulnerable to Indians armed with muskets, requested Plymouth as the biggest and strongest settlement to suppress Merry Mount. Bradford issued two warnings first, and then sent Standish with an armed force. The result was high comedy; Morton and his men stood to the defence and Standish waited. Then the rogues staggered out to attack the besiegers but they were too drunk to lift their muskets to their shoulders and all was over. Morton was put in prison at Plymouth until he could be sent to England, the better types were found employment and the others sent packing.

Allerton was in England again that winter. While the results of his previous visit had been generally satisfactory there had been some difficulties. He had brought over another priest, called Rogers, but he turned out to be 'crased in his braine' and had to be sent home again at a cost that could be ill-spared. Allerton had also brought some goods of his own for trade, which caused much confusion and annoyance. But he was a senior member of the community, he had married Fear, Brewster's daughter, two years before, and he was sent off again with strict instructions: no private trade, a better patent for the Kennebec, and a passage for the rest of the Leyden people if possible. He found Sherley sympathetic; indeed he declared that if persecution or trouble in England grew worse he would join them himself in the New World. (That year King Charles had called his third Parliament and the two sides were already at each other's throats; the first verbal battles of the Civil War were being fought.)

1629: THE LAST SAINTS ARRIVE

Sherley had been in Holland for three months and organised the Leyden exodus. Passages were found for the emigrants in ships bound for Salem, a few in the *Mayflower* (not the original ship) and more in the *Talbot*. Among these forty-five newcomers were Kenelm, Edward Winslow's younger brother, and Thomas Blossom, one of the original *Speedwell* passengers who had turned back at old Plymouth. It cost the Pilgrims over £550 ($1,300) to bring them across the Atlantic, apart from fetching them from Salem to Plymouth, but the migration was now virtually complete. A few more stragglers were to arrive over the next few years, among them Isaac Robinson, the first pastor's son.

The exodus which had begun in the Midlands of England in 1607, and which had been resumed from Holland in 1620, reached its conclusion by 1630. Though the new Canaan was no land flowing with milk and honey it would support those who were willing to work for their food, it was developing, the language and customs were English, and above all the country was free from the oppression of kings and bishops. But the battle against this oppression was developing fast in England, other eyes were being cast across the Atlantic, and the years that saw the Leyden community finally brought together in the New World saw a new wave of settlers on a scale that within a century would submerge the pioneer Plymouth colony.

CHAPTER SEVEN

The Old Colony

IN THESE FIRST FEW YEARS in which the Pilgrims were struggling to establish themselves in America there was no lack of propaganda in England to urge others to follow them. They themselves did not seek to hide the difficulties they had to face. What is known as *Mourt's Relation*, although actually written by Bradford and Winslow, was published in London in 1622, and Winslow's *Good Newes from New England* followed two years later. Both were designed to bring more people to Plymouth and both give honest accounts of all the initial hardships. Captain John Smith was also at work and his *New England's Tryalls* of 1622 set out in glowing terms the riches that the summer fishermen were bringing home, and the number of beaver skins exported; how much more could be done if people were settled on the coast, he argued, instead of wasting half the season traversing the Atlantic. That year too the Council of New England published their *Brief Relation of New England* which, after recounting the history of the various plantations, held the land up as the golden mean, with an agreeable and healthy climate; good soil; convenient harbours; well-wooded; tractable natives; and plentiful fish, wildfowl and game; and for potential trade the furs, three kinds of native wine, iron ore and all the necessities for building and rigging ships.

Extracts from all these writings were included in the volumes which the Rev Samuel Purchas was steadily publishing, continuing the work of the great Elizabethan Hakluyt in recording the important English voyages. *Purchas His Pilgrimes* had a steady sale; Emmanuel Altham in a 1623 letter from Plymouth wrote that he had asked his brother to 'buy me the books of English voyages . . . that is lately put forth by Mr Purchas, minister about Ludgate'.

One of the people influenced by this propaganda was the Rev John White, vicar of Dorchester in south-west England. After 1622,

Page 125 (*above*) The first Thanksgiving is enacted at Plimoth Plantation. Note the turkey hanging from the tripod; (*below*) Leyden Street today, on the site of the original settlement, looking from the shore up to Town Square with its two churches

Page 126 Plimoth Plantation: (*above*) the village under snow; (*below*) a kitchen in one of the houses, with a chicken cooking on a turnspit.

when the first three books were published, he became a firm advocate of settlement in New England. He was a conforming Puritan with no desire to break from the Church of England, but he had a liberal outlook and felt that a church set up in the New World would be free from the pressures already mounting in the old. He formed a company of fishermen from the Dorset coast whom he sent out to Cape Ann in 1624. They were able to help the Plymouth men in the fishing-stage dispute there, but these fishermen were no more successful as settlers than the Plymouth men as fishers, and the colony broke up in 1626. It was not a complete failure, for some of them moved down the coast to start afresh at Salem. Their leader was Roger Conant from East Budleigh in Devon, who had arrived at Plymouth as a 'particular' in 1623 but had later moved to join the Rev John Lydford when Plymouth expelled him.

In England the Rev John White continued to press his ideas. He was a product of Winchester and Oxford, with links with the great world. One of his converts had marriage links with the Gorges and with the family of the Earl of Lincoln, one of whose household had obtained the first Pilgrim patent and had planned to go with them. A Lincoln daughter, Lady Arabella, was married to Isaac Johnson and these two became leading spirits in a New England Company formed in 1628.

Just as the accession of King James I in 1603 produced the religous intolerance which sent the Scrooby congregation to Leyden, so the succession of his son Charles I in 1625 produced new pressures. By plunging into war with Spain he strained the nation's economy; by his taxes to pay for the war he fell out with his Parliaments, and the burdens on the taxpayers were a trial even to his potential supporters. The cost of living began to rise. Even the Puritans among the gentry whose sympathies were with Parliament could see that the belligerence of its members must end in a head-on clash. The old comfortable life of the landowners was in danger. So the Rev John White found an audience in a higher strata of society than had hitherto shown any interest in going overseas.

The New England Company at once sent out a party, under Captain John Endecott (another Devon man, from Chagford) to reinforce the Salem settlement. Early in 1629 the King finally fell out with his Parliament; it stood dissolved and its leaders (chief among them John Eliot from St Germans, just a few miles from old Plymouth) were in the Tower of London. All that summer there was a series of meetings at Sempringham, the seat of Lord Lincoln, near Boston. A parson from there was sent out to Salem, and the Massachusetts Bay Company was formed to take over from the New England Company; nine of the former Plymouth Plantation adventurers were shareholders. A patent was obtained from the king for a settlement across the Atlantic, and by August the promoters, meeting now at Cambridge, resolved that they would settle there by 1 March 1630. In October, at another Cambridge meeting at which the Rev John White was present, a lawyer called John Winthrop was brought into the discussions. He was a Puritan, a country gentleman from Suffolk, a lawyer with a promising career before him. Now he had been dismissed by the king from his appointment as a draughtsman of Parliamentary Bills. He had lost an income of £700 (nearly $1,700) a year and knew from his work in Whitehall just how deep the division in the country was. Five days later he accepted an invitation to become governor of the new plantation.

The king thought he had granted approval to just another trading company but these men had already resolved that the financial backing and the control would not this time remain in England. The whole group was emigrating, and taking the royal charter with them; they would be governed by themselves in the New World.

The company bought one ship, the *Eagle*, which they renamed *Arabella* in honour of her most distinguished passenger, and she became the flagship of a fleet of ten vessels (including yet another *Mayflower*) which sailed from Southampton the following March. The fleet carried over 700 men, women and children, drawn from all over England but chiefly from Suffolk, Essex and London. With the gentry there were twenty-five people over the rank of yeoman; the rest were tradesmen, artisans, and farmers, with their wives and families—a carefully balanced and selected company. There were two Suffolk parsons with them, and three of the Plymouth adventurers.

At about the same time the *Mary and John* sailed from old Plymouth with 150 people from Dorset, Devon and Somerset. Like the Southampton company it included two parsons, the Rev John Maverick, vicar of Beaworthy in Devon, and the Rev John Warham, vicar of St Sidwell's, Exeter. The Rev John White was in Plymouth to see them sail; he himself was too old for such a venture and indeed is remembered as 'the Patriarch of Dorset.' A friend of his, the Rev Matthias Nicholls was master of the Hospital of Poor's Portion, the new workhouse in Plymouth. There these new voyagers held a 'day of solemn prayer and fasting' and heard John White preach before they sailed. The granite archway through which they entered the building, with 'By God's helpe through Christ' carved on the lintel, still survives and has been re-erected in a garden at the back of New Street, just a stone's throw from the point whence the *Mayflower* sailed.

Both parties sailed at the right time of the year and made good voyages. They arrived 'in strawberry time'; there was fruit to combat any incipient scurvy and there was a welcoming colony established at Salem. From there the new people moved to the shores of Boston Harbour and soon new towns were springing up all round— Boston, Charlestown, Medford, Watertown and Roxbury. As might be expected, the Westcountry party named their town Dorchester. Not all happened at once; in spite of the careful preparations and adequate capital it was a raw new world. Winthrop's son Henry was drowned a day or two after arrival when trying to swim; neither Lady Arabella nor her husband survived the first winter when scurvy made its almost inevitable appearance. There was hunger, but at the worst a man could walk to Plymouth, as some did, and carry home corn for his family.

Plymouth and the new settlers were on good terms. They had found Endecott and his pioneers men to their taste and, when scurvy hit the Salem people in their first winter, Samuel Fuller went over with his physic to doctor them. There he helped them organise the First Church of Salem on the Plymouth pattern. It was in the Massachusetts Bay ships that Plymouth was able to buy passages for the last of its brethren from Leyden. When a troublemaker called Billington (father of the problem boys of the first winter), a *Mayflower* passenger recruited in England and a one-time adherent of 'Mad Jack Oldham', was convicted of murder in Plymouth, Governor Bradford was glad to have a lawyer like Winthrop near at hand whom he could consult on the legality of the death sentence. It might be a pointer to the harsh and autocratic rule that Massachusetts was to enjoy that, where Bradford plainly had hesitated, Winthrop advised that the man should die and the land be purged from blood.

NEW PROSPERITY

The large settlement on Massachusetts Bay brought prosperity to Plymouth. From 1630 to 1640, as the troubles mounted in England and civil war loomed closer, so did more and more people move across the Atlantic. Between 1620 and 1642, 14,000 people emigrated from England to Massachusetts and practically all this influx to New England occurred after 1630. Mostly they came in summer and, as Plymouth had learnt from experience, it was sixteen months or more before they were growing their own food. So for that length of time each new wave had to buy provisions, and Plymouth, with its established cornfields and herds of cattle, enjoyed its first real prosperity. Early wills show a single cow valued at £20 ($48) against £10 ($24) for a house and garden. Plymouth began to spread with the demand for more land to be tilled.

A new charter had been obtained in 1630 from the Council of New England. It had only one weakness, that the king had not endorsed it. But it gave to William Bradford, his heirs and associates, all the land south of a line from the Cohasset River, which has its mouth just south of the bay which Boston dominates, to Narraganset Bay. There was some argument with the Bay Company, whose boundaries were equally vague, but the Plymouth colony was now a large area of which the town itself was just the capital.

The granting of 'great lots' to each family in 1627 had meant a series of farms set up round Plymouth Bay. At first servants or a son of the house tended the distant land, but as the demand for crops and cattle grew so the families began to move out to their farms. Originally they came in on Sundays for the collective church services but even this became difficult. In 1632, Miles Standish, John Alden, Jonathan Brewster, son of the elder, and Thomas Prence (a 'stranger' who had arrived in the *Fortune* in 1621 and married Patience Brewster two years later), asked if they could form their own church at Duxbury. Standish named the new town after his English home near Chorley in Lancashire. Later William Brewster joined his children there, and Stephen Hopkins moved into Duxbury as well. Duxbury was recognised as a separate town of the colony in 1637. The year before Edward Winslow had moved to Marshfield and that in time became another town, with its own church.

Other towns were growing in the colony. Some of the London adventurers had bought land at Scituate from the Indians in 1628 and settled some men from Kent there. In 1634 they were joined by the minister and forty-two members of the Separatist church of Southwark. With the steady inflow of Puritans into the Bay colony some moved across into Sciutate, and in 1637 that too became a separate town. It was in fact to grow into the richest town of the colony, while Plymouth itself stayed a small town deprived of its chief citizens. It too had been changing steadily. After 1628 thatch was forbidden, to cut down the fire risk, and chimneys were increasingly built of brick. The bricks, which at first arrived as ballast, were soon being made locally, but wood was still, as now, the basic building material.

Not only Plymouth town but its founding fathers were suffering in spite of the prosperity. Allerton had defied instructions and continued trading on his own account. He had particularly annoyed his colleagues in 1629 by bringing back Thomas Morton as his clerk, the very man whom they had had to turn out of Merry Mount by force of arms. Plymouth soon turned him out again and off he went to the Bay, where a warrant for his arrest from England overtook him and he was sent back for a long spell in Exeter Prison. But he talked his way out of that, and published a scurrilous book, *New England Canaan* which held Plymouth and its people up to ridicule.

More serious, Allerton's mismanagement of their affairs while he lined his own pockets meant that those who had shouldered all the debts of the colony found that their liabilities in England, instead of being paid off, had grown from £400 ($950) to £4,000 ($9,500) in a few years. Not until 1648 was this original debt on the colony paid off. They had shipped £20,000 ($47,600) worth of beaver skins before they cleared what had started as a debt of

£1,800 ($4,300), and even then Winslow and Bradford had to sell their houses to clear off the last debts. This is one historian's interpretation, but the figures are inextricably involved and another study suggests that the original investors only received about a third of their capital back.

Allerton would bring in a load of goods needed in the colony. What he could sell went to his account; what he could not sell went into the general store and he said that it belonged to the community. He bought another fishing boat in spite of Plymouth's many failures in that trade. Even more unsatisfactory, he and his London friends (now largely shipping out of Bristol) obtained a patent for more land in Maine and set up a trading post at the mouth of the Penobscot, on the site of the modern Castine. Plymouth was pressed into taking a share in this, although they did not like Ashley, the young man brought over to take charge. To watch him they installed their own man, Thomas Willet, who had arrived from Leyden in 1629. Allerton and his friends also set up, completely on their own account, another trading post at Machias, even further north-east in Maine and provocatively close to the French.

Ashley soon came to a bad end; he was found to be selling weapons to the Indians, 'had comited uncleannes with Indean women', and was sent off to the Fleet prison in London. With difficulty Plymouth prevented all his store of beaver skins being confiscated as well. Allerton was dismissed as the company's business man early in 1631 and after that the Penobscot post passed entirely into Plymouth's control and under Willet began to prosper. But that summer the French moved, killing two men at Machias and taking all Allerton's store of skins. A little later a French ship appeared off the Plymouth post at Penobscot, and by a trick stole £400 ($950) or £500 ($1,300) worth of trading goods and 300 lb of beaver skins. In 1633 another trading post was established on the Connecticut River, at the invitation of the Indians but to the annoyance of the Dutch, who first tried to bar their passage.

It is indicative of the spreading of the old colony that in the spring of the next year, 1634, Thomas Prence of Duxbury was elected governor. Winslow had succeeded Bradford the previous

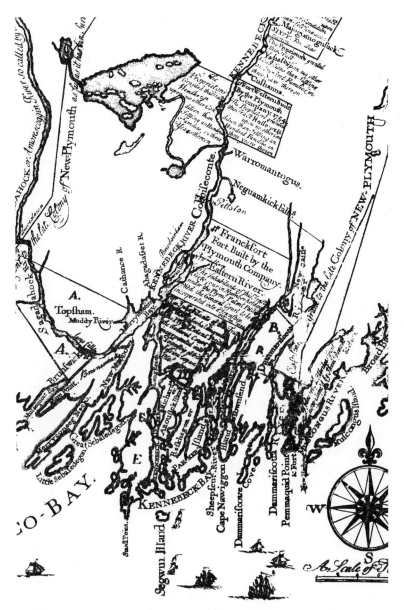

Details from a map in the Massachusetts state archives lodged in support of an eighteenth century land claim and showing the extent of the land granted to the Plymouth Colony on either side of the Kennebec River, in Maine

year, and these three men were to share the office until the last survivor, Prence, died in 1673. But more trouble at the most succesful trading post, on the Kennebec, came in 1634. A boat from Strawberry Banke, now Portsmouth, New Hampshire, came up under the command of a man called Hocking, with the intention of installing a trading post higher up the river. The men at the Plymouth post knew only too well that the highest trading post commanded the Indian trade; that was why they had gone above the fishermen in Maine and the Dutch on the Connecticut. Their title to the Kennebec was sound and they would not let Hocking pass. When he insisted, a canoe was sent out with two men to cut the boat's anchor cable and send it downstream on the current. Hocking shot and killed one of the men in the canoe; the other man shot back and killed Hocking.

The interlopers took their version of the story back to their base, whence word reached Massachusetts. There was much concern, for now Archbishop Laud was in power in England. Not only was he a scourge to the Puritans at home but he was head of a commission to regulate trade, religion and civic matters in the plantations. Hocking was a servant of Lord Saye and Sele, one of the Anglican Council of New England, and the Puritans in America were having to watch their step. When John Alden called at Boston on a supply voyage from the Kennebec he was arrested and imprisoned by the Bay officers. Plymouth sent Standish to protest that they were exceeding their authority, which did not run either to Plymouth or to the Kennebec. Alden was released but Standish in turn found himself bound over to produce the Plymouth title to the Kennebec. Receiving further protests from Plymouth, Winthrop proposed that a joint commission from Plymouth, Boston and the northern settlements should examine the matter. Plymouth agreed reluctantly, and all was smoothed over.

Winslow went to England that autumn as agent, with a cargo of skins that fetched nearly £4,000 ($9,500), and also to clear Plymouth with Lord Saye and Sele, and with the Commissioners of the Plantations. This he succeeded in doing, defeating a plan of Gorges to revive his claim to all New England. But Morton, the old enemy of Merry Mount, was put up to complain about the conduct of civic and religious affairs at Plymouth. In spite of Winslow's vigorous defence, Archbishop Laud sent him to the Fleet prison, where he lay for seventeen weeks before his release was secured.

1635 was not a good year for Plymouth. The French sailed into their trading post at Castine, in Maine, turned out Willet by force, and took over the post. Plymouth hired a well-armed 300 ton ship from the Bay to turn out the French, and Standish went as well with an armed party in a smaller vessel. But the big ship shot off her guns at too great range, wasted her powder, and failed to move the French. Standish came home empty-handed, and Plymouth was later infuriated to find English ships, and even Bay merchants, trading with the enemy in what had been their post.

The Plymouth post on the Connecticut with Jonathan Brewster in charge flourished, but the next year John Oldham, the perpetual nuisance, set up with some Bay men at the present Wethersfield, below Hartford. Two years later almost the whole congregation of Westcountry people from Dorchester moved out of the Bay, driving their cattle before them along the narrow Indian trails through the forest, with the former Exeter parson, John Wareham, at their head. They founded Windsor, on the Connecticut. That year an Indian tribe killed nine men from the Wethersfield post and Massachusetts sent Captain John Endecott with a small force. They ran into such trouble that Plymouth was asked to help; in the end the Bay men managed without their neighbours, trapped and slaughtered a large force of Indians, and left the river open for development. More men from the Bay moved in and founded more towns. Massachusetts gave the Connecticut river towns their own government, as they did to another settlement at New Haven, on what is now the coast of Connecticut state. Plymouth had again been the pioneers but were not reaping the harvest; it cannot even have given them satisfaction to know that John Oldham had been knocked on the head with an Indian hatchet and killed in the fighting.

Plymouth, like the Dutch, continued trading on the Connecticut until the spread of farms and the growing towns took away all their Indian trade, and the post was given up. The Kennebec post was rented by a syndicate of Bradford, Prence, Willet and William Paddy until 1660 when the fall-off in the trade led Plymouth to sell their rights to a group of Boston men.

EXPANSION

All through the 1630s settlers were pouring into Massachusetts. Not all were content to accept the autocratic rule there, or the intolerant Puritan religion. Perhaps it was because Plymouth was settled without a pastor, and was a long time in finding one either to its taste or willing to settle, that the old colony was free from the intolerance and religious rancour which always beset Massachusetts. That colony from the start had a bevy of ministers and more flocked in, like the Rev Hugh Peters of Fowey in Cornwall. He went home at the start of the Civil War to become the great preacher to the army of Fairfax and Cromwell, and was later beheaded by Charles II for having preached the sermon which finally persuaded his father's judges to execute him. Some who arrived in Massachusetts left of their own accord, like the founders of Connecticut and New Haven; some were exiled and went north over the Massachusetts boundary into New Hampshire.

One who found no resting place in Massachusetts was the Rev Roger Williams. He had arrived at Boston with his wife in the *Lion*, the first supply ship for the Bay settlers, fresh from Cambridge and hot with ideas. Some of his doctrinal ideas upset Boston so much that when he was offered the pastorate at Salem the Bay people vetoed the appointment and Williams moved to Plymouth. Parsonless as usual, the colony welcomed him, but Bradford soon found him 'godly & zealous, but very unsettled in judgemente'. Plymouth could put up with his admonitions and reproofs from the pulpit, and even some of his wilder doctrinal ideas, but when he began to challenge the legality of their patent and their rights to govern, he had to go. So in 1633 Williams went off to Salem where even John Endecott fell under his spell. By October 1634 his seditious preaching was too much even for Salem, and he was given six weeks to 'depart out of this jurisdiction'.

He made a journey on foot in the bitter January of 1635 westward across Plymouth colony, to settle on the bank of the Seekonk, at the very edge of the Plymouth territory. A few poor outcasts joined him there but in the spring he was told by Plymouth, under pressure from Massachusetts, that he was within their jurisdiction and must move on. So Roger Williams and his friends crossed the

river and called their settlement Providence. His church is regarded
as the first Baptist church of America, but having suffered so much
he resolved that there would be complete freedom of worship
there. Others joined him, including the redoubtable Anne Hutchinson who was also turned out of Boston for her 'prophesying', and
the little state of Rhode Island which eventually grew up round
Providence always maintained its religious freedom.

The American seaboard was filling up. In 1632 King Charles
gave his father's old Secretary of State, Lord Baltimore, a 'palatinate'
round the head of Chesapeake Bay. His son actually settled it in
1635 and called it Maryland in honour of the queen. Because he
was a Catholic, Lord Baltimore proclaimed freedom of religion
there, and in spite of Virginian opposition the colony eventually
flourished.

In 1638 the Dutch on the Hudson River found some interlopers
in what they regarded as their territory. The Protestant Swedes
had founded a settlement at what is now Wilmington, at the head
of Delaware Bay. Virginia also claimed this territory but they were
too far off to do much; the Dutch argued and protested but the
Swedes settled firmly into what is now the state of Delaware and
not until 1655 did the Dutch take it over.

Plymouth colony too was filling up. Men from Massachusetts
reached down past Plymouth town to settle on Cape Cod Bay,
founding Sandwich in 1637, and Barnstable and Yarmouth soon
after. Another group from Boston reached inland to found a settlement in 1630 where the old trail from Plymouth to Massasoit's
base crossed a big river. They were joined in 1637 by Elizabeth
Pole and her brother William, with their servants. They were very
different from the usual run of settlers in Plymouth colony, for
their father was Sir William Pole of Shute in east Devon, a distinguished lawyer and antiquary and of ancient descent. What
induced this 48 year-old spinster and her brother to leave home is
unknown; the rest of her family found life endurable in England,
and they were under no apparent religious or political pressure.
At any rate Elizabeth Pole walked through the woods from Boston
with the servants driving their cattle; they bought a large tract of
land which they called Taunton, and named the river the Taunton
River. When iron ore was found there Elizabeth, a woman of

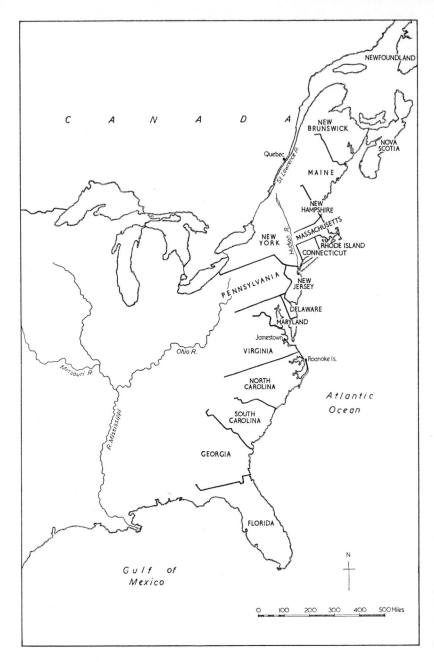

Sketch-map of the eastern seaboard of the United States. At the time of the Declaration of Independence, Florida was still Spanish, Maine was part of Massachusetts, and New Brunswick and Nova Scotia, originally settled by the French as Acadie, were part of Canada

wealth, contributed handsomely towards the capital needed to set up the Taunton iron works, the colony's first industry. Her old home at Shute in Devon is now a girls' school and the present head of the family, Sir John Carew-Pole, lives just across the Tamar River from old Plymouth at Antony House.

But with Plymouth colony becoming so widespread the old town meeting to run affairs was no longer feasible. In 1636 it had been necessary to draw up what was virtually a constitution for the colony, whose basic principles were that no laws might be made or taxes levied without the consent of the freemen or their elected representatives; that the governor and his assistants be elected annually; that the rule of law should prevail and trial by jury be open to all men; and that the church should be protected and each town provide for its ministers. Three years later it was agreed that the administration should be by a general court, to which each town sent two members, and Plymouth town five. The original freemen were the signers of the Mayflower Compact in Province-town Harbour in 1620. More freemen were admitted in subsequent years; they had to be over 21, settlers, and of good reputation. When the new towns were created each applicant had to be approved by his neighbours before the general court considered his claim. Thus Plymouth was democratic from the start, even if not in the modern 'one man one vote' idea, and for major decisions the whole body of freemen would meet together.

THE CIVIL WAR

The expansion of the colony met a check in 1641 with the out-break of the Civil War in England. Some men from Massachusetts went home to take part in the struggle, on either side, but the colonies stayed neutral. The main blow was that the flow of emigrants was halted. Plymouth was particularly hard hit, for it had come almost completely to depend on the trade of feeding new-comers until they could establish themselves. The price of corn fell to nothing and a cow was worth less than a quarter of what had been the prevailing price. The fur trade had been let slip; not only was it becoming increasingly competitive and difficult, but feeding the newcomers had become more profitable.

So Plymouth, like its Massachusetts neighbours, turned to trading with the West Indies. These islands and Barbados had attracted over 36,000 immigrants before the war compared with the 14,000 who went to New England, they were wealthy, and they needed the temperate foodstuffs and timber which New England had in abundance. Boston ships provided the main but not the only carriers and the New Englanders had to learn deep-water voyaging. The navigation was not difficult: Admiral Morison quotes the old captain who explained the basic principle as 'sail south till your butter melts, then west.'

For Plymouth town it was a particularly difficult time. The old leaders had moved out and more were going, the town had a long argument with a new minister about the rites of baptism, drunkenness was appearing, and sexual offences and deviations. The leaders, old men now, were hunting the Scriptures to find the right punishments for adultery, sodomy and bestiality. A simple farm labourer from Duxbury was executed for the latter crime but one doubts if there was really very much of any of this; that it even existed at all in their midst was grievous to them.

An even greater blow came on 18 April 1643 when William Brewster died, 'a man that had done and suffered much for ye Lord Jesus'. In his History, Bradford set down his sorrowing obituary, recounting the years of high office under Secretary Davison in the Low Countries, holding possession of the keys of Flushing and awarded by the States with a gold chain which he wore about his neck on his return to England. He had gathered the first church round him in Scrooby, he had suffered most imprisonment in the attempts to leave the country, and after spending his own means in getting the pilgrims to Leyden he had recouped by teaching English at the university. In the New World he had preached twice every Sunday when there was no minister and led the prayers, managed the affairs of the church wisely and compassionately, and yet had worked daily in the fields till his old age. He was 80 when he died.

One effect of the Civil War in England was to join the colonies closer together. Though they all felt themselves independent of each other they had previously been able to look to England as a central authority; they had all removed themselves from that parental control but its existence afforded some comfort. Now, the country split between two warring armies ('those distractions in England', Bradford in his History called the war, just as the English during World War II kept talking about the 'emergency'), the plantations could only look to themselves, and the Indians were still restless after the slaughter in Connecticut. So articles of confederation were signed between Massachusetts, Plymouth, Connecticut and New Haven. Each was to keep its own jurisdiction but they entered upon a permanent league of friendship and amity. If any were to be attacked the rest would send help, Massachusetts a hundred armed men and the others forty-five each. It gives a sharp picture of the relative strengths; the oldest colony was no more populous now than the youngest. More men could be called out if needed. Two commissioners from each colony were to meet at least annually, elect a president from their ranks, and direct the business of the confederacy. The annual meetings were to be held at Boston, Hartford, New Haven and Plymouth, in that order, unless some suitable central point were agreed on.

Plymouth was placed last in those 1643 plans. It was in danger of being abandoned altogether. Seeing that so many people were moving away, the church considered whether a complete move was not desirable, rather than this constant draining of its strength. Nauset, the present Eastham across the bay from Plymouth on Cape Cod, was a suggested site, and a number did in fact move. The others changed their mind and stayed, but it was a much depleted community. Bradford, who alone of the original leaders of the Pilgrims had stayed in Plymouth, wrote:

> . . . thus was this poore church left, like an anciente mother growne olde, and forsaken of her children. . . . Her anciente members being most of them worn away by death; and these of later times being like children translated into other families, and she like a widow left only to trust in God. Thus she that had made many rich became her selfe poore.

Even Edward Winslow, who went to England on the colony's business, accepted employment by Cromwell and considerable preferment in the Commonwealth after the Civil War. He was eventually sent as chief civil commissioner on an expedition led by Admiral Sir William Penn to the West Indies which resulted in

England taking possession of Jamaica. But Winslow died and was buried at sea on the homeward voyage in 1655. He was about 61.

In the following year Miles Standish died at Duxbury, aged 72. Only ten years earlier he had been out in command of the Plymouth soldiers in the first confederacy force against the Indians. Though he is remembered as a soldier and a fiery little man he was a stalwart of the colony in other ways, always urging toleration, serving as treasurer and assistant governor at various times. He left the largest estate in the colony up to that time and a remarkable little library, including Caesar's *Commentaries*—a wise choice, for the woad-painted Britons who opposed the Romans were not dissimilar to the Indians whom the first soldiers of New England had to fight. His massive monument still looks down from Captain's Hill at South Duxbury, watching over Plymouth as Standish himself did in the vital years.

The next year death took the greatest of the Plymouth leaders, William Bradford. He had succeeded Carver as governor when the colony was a few months old, and when he died in 1657, aged 67, he had just completed his thirtieth term in the office. If Brewster, his father-figure and mentor in far-away Scrooby all those years before, was the religious inspiration of the Pilgrims in the New World, his protégé Bradford was the civic. He had brought the young colony through its years of difficulty with the Indians and the adventurers in England, he had shouldered the burdens of office and the debts of the foundation, and played a full part in forming the confederacy. After surrendering so much of his own for the good of his fellows it is pleasant to see that his last years were comfortable. He had rented the Kennebec trading post from the colony and the fur trade had prospered. He had silver and Venetian glass on his table, 300 books on his shelves, and a 300 acre farm round the orchards and gardens of his Plymouth house. His estate when he died was valued at £900 (over $2,100), making him the colony's richest man. For posterity his richest legacy was his history of the colony.

Isaac Allerton, whose trading methods had caused Bradford so much trouble, died two years later in New Haven after having moved from colony to colony. He left a pile of debts which more than swallowed up his estate.

Page 143 Plymouth, Mass, today (*above*) schoolchildren on Cole's Hill with the Massasoit statue looking down at the canopy over the Rock and the masts of *Mayflower II* over the trees. Clark's Island with Plymouth Beach in front of it is seen over the canopy; (*below*) *Mayflower II* at State Pier

יהוה עזר היי

Under this stone
rest the ashes of
WILL^M BRADFORD
a zealous puritan &
sincere christian
Gov. of Ply. Col. from
April 1621 to 1657,
(the year he died
aged 69)
except 5 yrs.
which he declined.

Qua patres difficillime
adepti sunt nolite
turpiter relinquere

Page 144 Plymouth, Mass, today (*above*) looking from Burial Hill across Town Square to Manomet Heights; (*below*) Main Street, looking past the seventeenth century Howland House over Town Brook to Burial Hill; typical small towns in New England

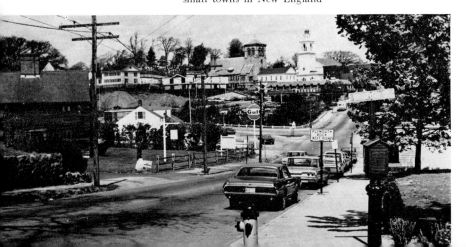

Thomas Prence succeeded as governor with John Alden, the cooper from Southampton who still worked as a carpenter, as his principal assistant. But among the leaders now were the second generation, Josiah Winslow, William Bradford the younger and his two stepbrothers, Thomas and Constant Southworth. Thomas Cushman, son of the Cushman who had organised the *Mayflower* voyage, had succeeded Brewster as deacon in 1643 and held that office for nearly fifty years.

NEW SETTLEMENTS

The new men had some sharp thinking to do in 1660 when Charles II was restored to the throne of England. Plymouth sent a declaration of loyalty. Three years later when a royal commission visited New England it reported favourably on the colony, and the contrary on Massachusetts. The Bay already had a royal charter, Plymouth now refused one because of the fear that in time it might bring a royal governor. Connecticut was given such a charter, bringing the river towns and New Haven into one colony, and even little Rhode Island, which had been studiously kept out of the Confederacy of New England because it insisted on freedom of religion, received one. Until then Rhode Island had only a Cromwellian charter granted in 1644. (Plymouth banished its Quakers to Rhode Island because they challenged civil as well as church authority; Massachusetts hanged them.)

King Charles was busy in the New World. In 1663 he gave charters to establish North and South Carolina as rewards to men who had supported his return to the throne. The next year he sent ships to drive Peter Stuyvesant and the Dutch from the Hudson. Their land he gave to his brother, the Duke of York, and New Amsterdam became New York. Thomas Willet, who had managed Plymouth's trading post on the Kennebec, became its first English mayor. All the coast from the Hudson to Delaware Bay the king gave to more proprietors, and they called it New Jersey. Land at the head of the Delaware was given to Sir William Penn and there his son, who had joined the Quakers, founded Pennsylvania in 1680 for his much-persecuted friends (map, page 138).

Although Plymouth was the smallest in population, and the

least well-off of the established colonies, it was still expanding. Fishing was developed on Cape Cod, and horse-rearing became important. More towns were founded. Rehoboth, (now in East Providence) across the Seekonk from Providence, had been sold to men from Massachusetts in 1643 and was admitted a town in 1645. Bridgewater was established by Duxbury men in 1656 to provide farms for their sons. Land on the north side of Buzzards Bay had early been given to Plymouth for cattle grazing but this was settled by people from Scituate, Marshfield and Sandwich in 1661, and recognised as the town of Rochester in 1686. Further west on this coast younger sons founded Dartmouth in 1664, and Little Compton in 1682, while Falmouth came into being in 1686. In many of these towns were Quakers and Baptists, like Isaac Robinson, (son of the Rev John Robinson of Leyden) who had to leave Barnstable because of his Quaker ideas and who founded Falmouth. Baptists from Rehoboth moved out to set up Swansea in 1667 (map, page 62).

KING PHILIP'S WAR

These towns in the west of the colony suffered badly in the last Indian war to trouble New England. Old Massasoit, friend of the early days, died in 1661. His sons had English names but his heir, Philip, resented finding the ancestral lands overrun by English towns. There was friction caused by cattle getting out of the farms into the Indian crops. He began to store arms. An Indian, educated at Harvard (founded at Boston as early as 1636) and a preacher to the Indians converted to Christianity, warned Plymouth in 1674 of Philip's warlike intentions. This Indian was murdered; Plymouth found three of Philip's men guilty of the murder and executed them. Next year Philip launched an all-out attack through Plymouth colony. Massachusetts men joined the Plymouth colony soldiers; other Indian tribes joined Philip, and the infant colonies knew real war. Josiah Winslow, Edward's son, became commander-in-chief; there were marches and counter-marches, ambushes, Indian raids right close in to the biggest settlements, fire, massacre and torture for the outlying towns. Mothers dared not let children out of their sight; men not away soldiering stayed close to their farms, and all the towns kept a 24 hour watch. All the colonies were in peril. Peace did not come to Plymouth until the summer of 1676, when Captain Benjamin Church, a Duxbury man who had moved to Little Compton, led a force which stormed Philip's central base at Mount Hope, his father's old village on the east coast of Bristol, Rhode Island. Philip was killed and his head set up on a pole over Plymouth; soon after that fight the rest of his force surrendered.

New Hampshire and Maine did not know peace for another two years; much of the settled land away from the coast in Massachusetts and in Connecticut was not regained for forty years. A dozen towns had been destroyed, another forty damaged, and over 500 men of military age killed. Plymouth suffered less than the other colonies because it had converted more Indians to Christianity and the 'praying Indians' did not rise. Even so the taxes levied on her towns fell from £3,692 ($8,787) before the war to £203 ($483) the year after, a guide to the damage done. There had been no help for New England from the old country or from the southern colonies, not even from New York; Virginia even stopped selling the New Englanders foodstuffs. But there was never again an Indian problem; though the Indian women and children were left alone the male prisoners were sold off as slaves away from New England. It was felt that their savagery in the war to English women and children, and to men whom they had captured, put them beyond the pale.

Plymouth felt so secure that the old fort on Burial Hill was pulled down. Its function as a church had ended years before, in 1648, when a separate meeting house had been built in Town Square, looking down Leyden Street. Harlow Old Fort House, which still stands half a mile south of the square, was built in 1677 and tradition says that the timbers of the old fort were incorporated in it.

INDEPENDENCE LOST

For the brief reign of James II Plymouth colony found itself part of the Dominion of New England under a royal governor in Boston but, like the other colonies, re-asserted its independence in 1689 when the news came that William of Orange had chased King James out of England. Now Plymouth tried to get a royal charter from the new sovereign, but all the colonies were busy

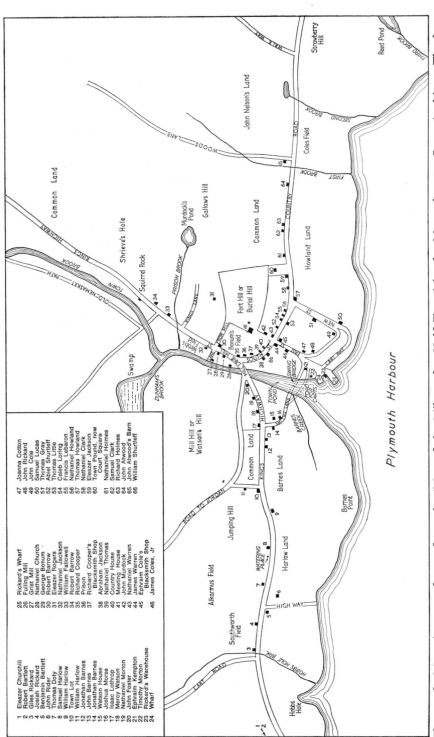

Plymouth, Mass, in 1701, drawn from the 'Map of the Mile and a Half Tract' in the Massachusetts State Archives. The key gives each householder and identifies the industrial and public buildings, and shows the development of the town within a

1	Eleazer Churchill
2	Robert Bartlett
3	Giles Rickard
4	Josiah Rickard
5	Benjamin Bartlett
6	John Rider
7	Thomas Doty
8	Samuel Harlow
9	William Harlow
10	Town Lot
11	William Harlow
12	Jonathan Barnes
13	John Barnes
14	Jonathan Barnes
15	Watson House
16	Joshua Morse
17	Isaac Lothrop
18	Mercy Watson
19	Nathaniel Morton
20	John Foster
21	Ephraim Kempton
22	Timothy Morton
23	Rickard's Warehouse
24	Wharf
25	Rickard's Wharf
26	Fulling Mill
27	Grist Mill
28	Nathaniel Church
29	George Bonum
30	Robert Barrow
31	Eleazer Rogers
32	Nathaniel Jackson
33	William Fallowell
34	Robert Barrow
35	Richard Cooper
36	Prison
37	Richard Cooper's Blacksmith Shop
38	Abraham Jackson
39	Nathaniel Thomas
40	Country House
41	Meeting House
42	John Murdock
43	Nathaniel Warren
44	James Warren
45	Ephraim Cole's Blacksmith Shop
46	James Coles, Jr
47	Joanna Cotton
48	John Rickard
49	John Cole
50	Samuel Lucas
51	Thomas Gray
52	Abiel Shurtleff
53	Thomas Little
54	Caleb Loring
55	Francis Lebaron
56	Nathaniel Howland
57	Thomas Howland
58	Nathaniel Clark
59	Eleazer Jackson
60	Town Pound, now Court Square
61	Nathaniel Holmes
62	Samuel Clark
63	Richard Holmes
64	John Atwood's Barn
65	John Atwood
66	William Shurtleff

lobbying in London. The strong colonies saw a chance to expand. New York had already persuaded the king to give it Long Island. Perhaps it amused Dutch William to see the expansion of what had been a Dutch colony. Emboldened by this eastern extension, New York was also asking for Cape Cod and the islands to the south, and all Plymouth colony. Massachusetts was also asking for Plymouth.

The Old Colony was between the devil and the deep blue sea. She had never had a royal charter, and this was her undoing. Such charters that existed were respected by William and Mary; even little Rhode Island, and New Hampshire which had only won independence from Massachusetts in 1680, kept their independence. Plymouth fought in vain; in the end it was clear that she must choose, and she finally plumped for Massachusetts. She was better off under Boston rule than that of New York, for in spite of all their differences the motivating spirit of Massachusetts and Plymouth had always been the same. So, in 1691, the oldest colony of all lost its independence and became a part of Massachusetts. In the next century the western towns of Plymouth Colony, on the shores of Narragansett Bay and the Seekonk river, passed to Rhode Island, and the Old Colony merged into the general stream of American history.

Only one more colony, Georgia, was to be established. James Oglethorpe obtained a patent in 1732 to settle there, his aim being to provide a new life for the debtors who crowded the English prisons. There was to be religious freedom (save for Catholics), no hard liquor and no slaves. The settlers were not all insolvent; the young John and Charles Wesley were among them though they only stayed two years. The Carolinas welcomed the new men, who formed a buffer against the Spanish still in Florida (map, page 138).

The Anglo-French wars which raged for most of this century ended with the 1763 Treaty of Paris which gave all Canada to England, leaving the French only their settlements around the mouth of the Mississipi, the present New Orleans and Louisiana. Now in possession of the whole eastern seaboard of North America, England sought to strengthen her control. The English colonies resisted this for they were now free of the threats from the French who had been reaching out from Canada and Louisiana to link up behind them. Above all they resented taxation imposed by the English Parliament in which they had no voice, even though it was being imposed to pay the debts of a war which had given them this new freedom from fear. As the argument developed, with Boston and Massachusetts to the forefront on the American side, the colonies drew together and in 1774 held their first Congress. Two years later, on 4 July 1776, the Declaration of Independence was signed. In September 1783 Britain had lost the long war and recognised the independence of the United States.

If Plymouth in her early days had gained a royal signature to one of her charters she would have been the fourteenth founding state. Maine, which had also been swallowed up by Massachusetts, won statehood in 1820. But the Old Colony remained divided into five counties, Plymouth, Barnstable and Bristol in Massachusetts; Newport and Bristol in Rhode Island. Plymouth colony had grown from about 300 people in 1630 to over 3,000 by 1660, 5,000 by 1675 and between 12,000 and 15,000 when it was swallowed up by Massachusetts. In 1950 the five counties which occupied its territory had a total population of over 780,000, more people than a dozen other states of the Union and more than the population of Nevada, Delaware and Wyoming combined. The colony which the Pilgrim Fathers founded was independent only from 1620 to 1691. But it has not been forgotten.

CHAPTER EIGHT

Remembrance of Old Times

THE AWAKENING OF AMERICAN PATRIOTISM which led to the Declaration of Independence saw the dawn of Plymouth's pride in its ancestry. In January 1769 the Old Colony Club was founded by seven men, two Winslows and a Cushman among them, whose forebears went back to the earliest days. It was (and still is) a social club, founded because of 'the many disadvantages and inconveniences that arise from intermixing with the company at the taverns in this town'. By the end of the year they had resolved to celebrate the landing of their forefathers on 22 December. A cannon was fired, a silk flag inscribed 'Old Colony 1620' was hoisted on Old Colony Hall, and the members proceeded to the inn of Thomas Southworth Howland (which stood on the site of Plymouth's first tavern) where at 2.30 pm they sat down to a nine course dinner 'dressed in the plainest manner (all appearance of luxury and extravagance being avoided) in imitation of our ancestors'. There was whortleberry pudding, succatash (made from a complicated recipe which used various fowls and meats, corn, and so forth), clams, oysters and codfish, venison roasted on the first jack brought to the colony, sea fowl, frost fish and eels, apple pie, cranberry tarts, and local cheese. At 4 o'clock the members led by the steward carrying a folio volume of the laws of the Old Colony, walked in procession to the hall where a number of descendants from the first settlers, drawn up in file, greeted them with a volley of small arms and three cheers. The club responded with another three cheers, and schoolchildren sang a song 'very applicable to the day'. Possibly it was the 'Liberty Song', which is said to have been sung that day to the tune of 'Hearts of Oak'.

> Come join hand and hand brave Americans all
> And rouse your bold hearts at fair liberty's call.

The whole song is a poetical declaration of 'no taxation without representation'; subsequent years had specially-written hymns concerned more with ancestor-worship and less with revolution.

Plymouth Rock was already the symbol, the place of the very first landing. There was no doubt as to which rock it was. In 1741 the last ruling elder, Thomas Faunce, heard that a wharf was to be built on the Plymouth foreshore and although he was 95 he was carried in a chair three miles from his home to point out the Rock and explain that in his boyhood it had been generally regarded as the place where the forefathers, many of whom were still living then, had stepped ashore. Though the old man died twenty-five years before the Old Colony Club was formed, there were still people alive who had seen him point out the actual Rock. Two families cherished traditions that it was their ancestor who had first set foot upon it. The Aldens held it to have been John Alden, the Winslows that it had been Mary Chilton, a girl of 15 who seven years later had married John Winslow. In fact the first landing had been made by the exploring party which included neither Alden nor any women, but either could have been first ashore when *Mayflower* herself arrived in the harbour. There was also a date problem. The first landfall at Cape Cod was on 11 November, the first landing by the exploring party at Plymouth was on 12 December, another exploration was made on 17 December, and the main landing was on 18 December. But in 1752 Britain had adopted the Gregorian calendar to bring herself into line with Europe, jumping eleven days to catch up, to the disgust of the man in the street. So the first Plymouth landing, 12 December, was reckoned as 22 December.

However, the first Forefathers' Day in 1769 had finished with the Old Colony Club members sitting in their hall, with the president in Governor Bradford's old chair, drinking a series of twelve toasts which started with 'our brave and pious ancestors'. By the ninth they were proposing 'may every enemy to civil or religious liberty meet the same or a worse fate than Archbishop Laud'. He had been executed on Tower Hill, but the Old Colony members were not really breathing death to the British politicians. Their last toast was to 'a speedy and lasting union between Great Britain and her colonies'.

This was a view extensively held in New England, although the picture too often given of pre-Revolution days is of all Americans as devoted patriotic rebels. Many members of the older, established families, the landowners, had no wish to break with England even if they opposed its maladministration; when the break came many remained loyal to Britain as did Edward Winslow of Plymouth who in 1770 made the first of the long series of Forefathers' Day orations at the Old Colony Club celebrations. But America was changing; in the previous half-century the population had grown from 400,000 to 2,500,000. Most of these were from Scotland, Ireland and Germany, with no loyalty to England and no affection either for her or for the old families, whom they found dominating everything from industry to landownership on the eastern seaboard, and holding the financial strings of the interior as well. The masses were for revolution, and things like the death of four men in March 1770, when the British troops fired on a mob, became the 'Boston Massacre'. Politicians like Samuel Adams in Boston were quick to marshal these sentiments, and in no time ousted the old families from control there.

By 1773, a number of people in Plymouth suggested that Forefathers' Day celebrations should be opened to the whole town, and made a demonstration against British tyranny. This the Old Colony Club rejected, as they did again the following year. So in 1774 the people took things into their own hands. Led by Colonel James Warren, who had resigned from the club over this issue, and Colonel Theophilus Cotton, who two years later led the Plymouth Militia to help besiege the British in Boston as soon as news of the battle of Lexington was heard, the Plymouth Sons of Liberty took over Forefathers' Day for themselves:

In the year 1774 some ardent whigs, to render available the patriotic associations connected with the rock, undertook its removal to the town square, with the intention to place over it a liberty pole, as an excitment to vigorous efforts in the approaching revolutionary struggle, and to quicken the zeal of such persons as hesitated to join the standard of independence.

When they tried to move the Rock it split into two, which was

153

regarded as a favourable omen indicating the final separation of the colonies from England. The lower lump was left in place, the top part was hitched to twenty yoke of oxen and hauled off to the square to be 'honoured with the far-famed liberty pole, upon which an appropriate effusion of some patriotic son of liberty was placed'. They had 'made even our Tory protesters hang their ears', Colonel Warren wrote to Samuel Adams in Boston.

When war came Winslow's sons joined the British forces and he eventually had to leave his house on North Street for the British headquarters in New York, whence he moved on to Halifax, Nova Scotia, and died. Seven other members of the Old Colony Club joined the flow of loyalists to Nova Scotia (travel by sea was still easier than by land) and the club faded away, to revive in due course and remain hale and hearty on Main Street. Forefathers' Day went on as a popular event.

THE PILGRIM FATHERS

After the war Forefathers' Day was dropped for a few years, to be revived in the early 1790s when the minister of the First Plymouth Church, the Rev Chandler Robbins, preached from beside the Rock in Town Square. From the church records he took an extract from Bradford, describing the departure from Leyden, 'they knew they were pilgrims'. On that Forefathers' Day the term 'Pilgrim Fathers' was born. One verse of the hymn written for 1792 by the Hon John Davis and sung to the tune which also serves 'America' and 'God Save the Queen', finished with

> Hailing this votive day,
> Looking with fond survey,
> Upon the weary way
> Of Pilgrim feet.

The 1799 hymn, which was used for many years and sung to the music of 'Old Hundred', has as its first line

> Hail, Pilgrim Fathers of our race!

The term was firmly established. So was the business of the annual speech, and the specially-written hymn. John Quincy Adams, son of ex-President John Adams and destined himself to be the sixth President of the United States, delivered the 'anniversary discourse' in 1802 and wrote a hymn that morning when he got out of bed. It was sung at the celebrations the following year.

These sentimental songs, often using catchy popular tunes, did much to spread the Pilgrim mythology throughout the States. When the New England Club was formed in New York in 1807, there was a whole range of songs, full of 'Hail ye Pilgrims' and 'Hail sons of Pilgrims', and even a version of 'Yankee Doodle Dandy' telling the England-Leyden-America story. Not only New England, but all the northern Yankees were adopting the Pilgrims as their ancestors. In some ways there was justification; the move-on spirit of America was in Plymouth from the start and its sons and daughters spread steadily through the nation. Today the very name of Plymouth crops up thirty-five times across the country, from Florida to California.

With the approach of the second centenary of the landing there was a peak of interest, of the kind that has marked each centennial and bi-centennial year since. In 1819 the Pilgrim Society was formed with John Watson, one of the original seven founders of the Old Colony Club, as its first president. It was open to all who wished to honour the memory of the Pilgrims, and willing to pay an annual subscription of $10 (£4 3s od), later cut to $5 (£2 1s 6d). The intention was to erect 'durable monuments' at Plymouth. The actual anniversary was marked with a major ceremony at the Rock in Town Square at which the key speech was made by Daniel Webster, then a young lawyer in Boston who had bought Careswell, the old Winslow estate at Marshfield. With one spell in Congress behind him he was at the top of his powers; though the presidency was to elude him he was later to be twice secretary of state. By some he is held to be the greatest orator in American history, comparable with Demosthenes or Burke. Of his speech on 22 December 1820 it has been written 'in the line of general eloquence he never reached a greater height than this.' The Pilgrim Society had the speech printed and circulated.

Away in north Wales an English woman romanticist and writer of highly-popular sentimental ballads, Felicia Dorothea Hemans, found an account of a Forefathers' Day celebration in an old newspaper. The result was a poem, the 'Landing of the Pilgrims'. It became a party piece for generations of American schoolchildren.

> The breaking waves dashed high
> On a stern and rock-bound coast
> And the woods, against a stormy sky
> Their giant branches tost:

Mrs Hemans had never seen Cape Cod or Plymouth Bay, but she too played her part in the growth of the legend.

The Pilgrim Society laid the corner-stone of Pilgrim Hall in 1824, a classical granite temple which over the years became a museum of relics and pictures of the founding fathers, and a centre of research. In 1834 they acquired custody of the part of the Rock which was still leaning against the base of an elm tree in Town Square. It was moved on Independence Day with some ceremony, only marred when a wheel came off the cart and the Rock fell into the road. It broke yet again and the join still shows on the left-hand side of the top. It was set up in front of Pilgrim Hall with an iron fence to keep visitors off. The tourist trade had already started; some shopkeepers in the town were selling alleged pieces of the Rock.

It was the time of small ships and flourishing seaborne trade. Eight wharves reached out from Plymouth's waterfront between Town Brook and the modern State Pier, where *Mayflower II* is berthed. Clapboard sheds of all shapes and sizes covered this dock area, and in front of one such warehouse the flat top of the other half of the Rock made part of the road surface. Horses and carts with iron-shod wheels rumbled up and down over it; if a visitor showed interest a boy would come out of the warehouse to broom off the top of the Rock. The base of the wharf, with the Rock, was bought by the Pilgrim Society in 1859 and by demolishing some of the warehouses the Rock was at least given a little air and dignity.

A start was made to erect a classical canopy over it, and in 1867 the structure was completed. In the top were laid the bones of some of those who died in the first winter of 1621, and which had been found on Coles Hill close behind the Rock. But only half the Rock was so distinguished; not until 1880 was the top fetched out of its iron cage outside Pilgrim Hall and cemented back to its base. For years the top had carried the date 1620 in paint; now it was carved into the stone. (The most common question asked today by visitors looking down on the Rock is 'did the Pilgrims cut that date in it?') By 1883 the Pilgrim Society owned the whole wharf and it was cleared of buildings so that the canopy dominated the area. The wharf became the landing stage for the high-decked paddle-steamers bringing trippers and travellers down from Boston; the Rock stood before them as they arrived. To make sure that the travellers by sea did not overlook the significance of Plymouth the society erected the Pilgrim Monument, a vast erection of Quincy granite on a hill above the town. It was designed by Hammatt Billings, like the canopy over the Rock, and unveiled in August 1889. Though the modern traveller by road hardly sees the huge figure with upraised arm, it still looks bravely out to sea. The figure represents Faith, and round the plinth are plaques depicting events in the Pilgrim story.

THE BRADFORD HISTORY

Another spurt of interest in the last century came with the finding of William Bradford's History. He of course had been in the adventure from the start, and was governor from 1621 until 1656 with only five intervals of one year each. In 1630 he had started to write a full account of the colony, which he maintained until 1646, and made additions up to 1650. Various writers borrowed the manuscript from his descendants to use in their writings, even Increase Mather who, as Boston's bribing agent at the court of William and Mary, had done much to rob the old colony of its independence. Nathaniel Morton, Bradford's nephew and sometime secretary of the colony, copied the first forty-seven pages into the Plymouth church records.

But after the American Revolution, when the newly-independent nation began to look at its history (the Massachusetts Historical Society was founded in 1792) this vital book had disappeared. Only these extracts from it were known. Not until 1855 did an American writer, browsing through a book by the English Bishop Wilberforce in a Boston bookstore, recognise quotations from Bradford. From this the manuscript was tracked down to the library of the Bishop of London at Fulham Palace. A copy was made and for the first time Bradford's *Of Plymouth Plantation* was published in full, in 1856.

A note in the fly-leaf of the manuscript gives its history. Thomas Price, who had started putting together a New England library when he entered Harvard in 1702, had borrowed the manuscript from Bradford's grandson at Kingston in 1728, and had his permission to 'lodge it' in his library. On Price's death the books were all left to the Old South Church in Boston, where they were kept in the steeple. The loyalist Governor Hutchinson used it in his history of Massachusetts, published in 1767, but his house had been sacked in 1765 and he may have taken it with him when he left Boston with the British troops in 1766. A more popular belief is that when the British troops made Old South Church a riding school, before they had to evacuate the town, the book was looted from the steeple. But in some way it reached the Bishop of London, and it took forty years to persuade his Grace, and his consistory court, to part with it. Now it is back, not in Plymouth, but in a bronze and glass case in the museum of the Massachusetts state archives, in a basement of the golden-domed State House on Beacon Hill, Boston.

Bradford's History, available to scholars on both sides of the Atlantic after 1856, opened a new field. His clues to the origins of the Pilgrims set several researchers working through English parish registers and similar records, and piece by piece the early story was built up. In the second half of the century too the steamships were established on regular lines between America and Britain, and it became easy for Americans who claimed Pilgrim descent to visit their ancestral homes.

HOLLAND AND ENGLAND

The first such visit to make impact upon England and Holland, and to leave positive reminders, came in July 1891 when the first International Congregational Council was held in London. This strong and worldwide body of Nonconformists dates back to the first Separatists from the Church of England, and, of all its early exponents, John Robinson expressed the ideas most closely reflected in the modern church. But in the history of the church there have been splits, and two tablets in Town Square, Plymouth, Mass, tell the story quite succinctly. On the north side of the square is the white-painted Church of the Pilgrimage, with its pillared and domed belfry. Its tablet reads:

> This tablet is inscribed in grateful memory of the Pilgrims and their successors who at the time of the Unitarian controversy in 1801 adhered to the belief of the fathers and on the basis of the original creed and covenant perpetuated at great sacrifice in the Church of the Pilgrimage the evangelical faith and fellowship of the church of Scrooby, Leyden and the Mayflower organised in England in 1606.

On the east side of the square is the heavy stone First Church in Plymouth. Its plaque reads:

> The church of Scrooby, Leiden and the Mayflower, gathered on this hillside in 1620, has ever since preserved unbroken records and maintained a continuous ministry, its first covenant being still the basis of its fellowship. In reverent memory of the Pilgrim Fathers this fifth meeting house was erected A.D. 1897.

It was apparently a close vote in 1801 but the First Church joined the Unitarians. The minority broke away and built their own Congregational Church within a stone's throw: 'We kept the faith and they kept the furniture' as one bitterly expressed it.

The American Congregationalists who went to London in 1891 set out to stake their claim to the forefathers. There was after all a Dr Bradford among them, apart from Senator Patterson and Dr Dunning of Boston. They planned a pilgrimage to Leyden and the chairman of the Congregationalists of Plymouth, England, hearing this, invited them to visit Plymouth as well. A large tablet of bronze, presented by the National Council of the Congregational Churches of the United States and commemorating John Robinson and the Pilgrim Fathers, was unveiled on Pieterskerk in Leyden on 24 July. The party moved on to Plymouth, England, fifty-three strong, and apart from a number of public meetings and receptions they were shown the actual spot in Sutton Harbour from which the *Mayflower* had sailed.

Plymouth, like the rest of the country, was just waking up to the importance of its Elizabethan history. J. A. Froude's massive and many-volumed account of Tudor England had stirred this new interest and, soon after its last volume, there had appeared in Plymouth in 1871 the first two published histories of the town. There are earlier manuscript histories and terse versions of the town's story in earlier directories, but these two historians, Llewellyn Jewitt and R. N. Worth, are the first to deal with the *Mayflower*'s call at Plymouth. This must have been prompted by the books following the publication of Bradford's History.

Plymouth had been demonstrating its historical pride in durable stone. The new Guildhall of 1873 not only had towering statues of Drake and other heroes on its roof, but a series of windows depicting great events in its history, including the sailing of the *Mayflower*. The 1874 Mayor himself, Alfred Rooker, a deacon of Sherwell Congregational Church, gave the *Mayflower* window to the town. In 1884 a statue of Drake had been unveiled on Plymouth Hoe, and the tercentenary celebrations of the Armada in 1888 built up this ancestral pride. An Armada memorial was started on the Hoe, a little way from the Drake statue, with 'a bronze figure of Britannia on a lofty pedestal looking out over the waves she rules!' It had been unveiled only nine months before the American Congregationalists were shown by R. N. Worth the actual spot 'within a yard' from which their Pilgrim ancestors had sailed. With so many monuments going up it was not surprising that in 1891 it was 'this spot the Americans desired that the authorities should indicate by a memorial slab'. Within a month or two a granite paving stone engraved 'Mayflower 1620' was set in the middle of the West Pier of Sutton Harbour, with a bronze tablet set in the pier wall to explain the story. It could only be an approximate site, because a century earlier two piers had been built to protect the mouth of Sutton Harbour, and the western arm, now more often called the Mayflower Pier than anything else, had covered the old causey and flight of steps.

So Europe and England had acquired their first monuments to the Pilgrims. The Midlands birthplaces were not ignored; though the only evidence of interest is a report that in 1891 the font of Scrooby Church was sold to an American and the money put to the church restoration. It was an old font, replaced in an earlier restoration of 1864 when all the pews were ripped out as well. Two of these, with the running foliage carvings of the ancient Christian symbol of the vine, are still in the sanctuary at Scrooby and are called the Brewster Pews. A third is in Pilgrim Hall, Massachusetts.

One result of this 1891 tour was the return in 1896 of a party of twenty American Congregationalists, again led by Dr Dunning of Boston. The principal purpose of their visit was to watch the American ambassador in London lay the foundation stone in Gainsborough of the John Robinson Memorial Congregational Church. 'In memory of John Robinson, pastor and exile', says the stone, and the church is still busy though its late-Victorian redbrick building does not come off very well in comparison with the Georgian elegance of the neighbouring parish church of All Saints. At that time the Sturton-le-Steeple links of Robinson had not been tracked down and Gainsborough was regarded as his most likely birthplace. So it is a little ironic that Sturton today has no memorial to John Robinson while Gainsborough, with little claim to him, has a whole church. At the same time John Smyth, the leader of the Gainsborough Separatists, has no memorial in the town. No doubt Dr Dunning and his Congregational friends were aware that Smyth had finished up with the Baptists.

The very day, 29 June 1896, that the foundation stone was laid at Gainsborough the Americans also signed the visitors' book in the Church of St Helena, Austerfield, where William Bradford had been christened on 19 March 1589. The church was in great disrepair and little used or visited (one feels that there has not been much change in this respect, for the visitors' book of 1896 is still in use). That year another eighteen Americans signed the book, and a brass plate records the rebuilding of the south aisle of the church in 1897 by the Society of Mayflower Descendants and other citizens of the United States in memory of Governor Bradford. 'He was the first American citizen of the English race who bore rule by the free choice of his brethren', says the plaque. Outside, a painted board proclaims the church as 'dedicated to the mother of an Emperor: baptismal place of William Bradford, a founding father of a nation'. It is a proud boast for a little church, built about 1080 and still with a carved Norman arch over the porch. The world rather passes it by today, but its visitors' book does show a steady stream of American visitors.

The General Society of Mayflower Descendants who (no doubt moved by the Congregationalists) restored Austerfield Church, had only been formed the previous year. Membership is limited, as its name indicates, and tracing of descent has become a minor industry which the society promotes. Sixty years after its formation the society has established between 23,000 and 24,000 people in the lineage, of whom it now has about 16,000 active members and a Chapter in every state of the Union. Possibly its activity stirred the Pilgrim Society as well, for a bronze plaque, undated but apparently of about this time, was set up by them on the old Brewster home at the manor house in Scrooby.

The Congregationalists who went to Gainsborough and Austerfield in 1897 (they also visited Boston) had landed at Plymouth, and no doubt revisited the Barbican with its plaque marking their visit of five years before. Plymouth had since the arrival of the railway in 1849 been the first port of call by homeward-bound ships from the Far East. In 1893 the American Line moved its English terminus from Liverpool to Southampton and, like the French and German lines, began using Plymouth as their first eastbound call, because their passengers could save twenty-four hours by disembarking there and taking train to London, instead of going on up-Channel to Southampton. So the Mayflower Stone in Plymouth found itself on the Americans' route to London, and a convenient point of pilgrimage.

The Americans were becoming increasingly conscious of their ancestors. The Commonwealth of Massachusetts recognised 21 December as Forefathers' Day in 1895; President Abraham Lincoln in 1863 had appointed the last Thursday in November to be celebrated as Thanksgiving Day by a national holiday (it was changed in 1941 to the fourth Thursday). Places around Plymouth, Mass, became glad to mark their associations with the Pilgrims. The citizens of Gloucester, for instance, put up a tablet at Stage Fort Park in 1907 to mark the first settlement of the men from Dorchester, and also recorded on it the fact that the Pilgrims had trouble over their fishing-stage there. That year the British ambassador to Washington watched President Theodore Roosevelt lay the corner stone of the Pilgrim Memorial Monument at Provincetown, and in 1910 President Taft dedicated the 225 ft high tower which looks down over *Mayflower*'s first American anchorage. The Research Club of Provincetown was stimulated to study the early Pilgrim explorations, and in 1917 they began setting up markers to indicate the believed sites of the first landing and other key places.

Southampton, England, was becoming increasingly interested in Americans when the White Star Line transferred its American express-passenger services from Liverpool to that Channel port (Cunard did not follow until 1919). A local historian, F. J. C. Hearnshaw, wrote the *Story of the Pilgrim Fathers, especially showing the Connection with Southampton* in 1910, and in 1913 a memorial to the Pilgrims was erected there. The tall pillar surmounted by a crescent fire under a canopy, with a bronze *Mayflower* model above that, was built in front of the walls near the base of the Royal Pier, a compromise position half-way between the newly-built Ocean Dock where the Americans landed and the West Gate whence their ancestors sailed. (The Western Docks now completly cut West Gate from the sea, and dry land covers *Mayflower*'s anchorage). The American ambassador in London unveiled the memorial with its appropriate tablet on 15 August, and other tablets were added by the Alden Kindred of America, the descendants of Brewster and of Winslow. The memorial has become a repository for various other tablets since, including one to the American invasion forces of 1944 and even one to Blanche Butler Ford of the Colonial Dames of Ohio.

THE TERCENTENARY

The real international celebrations began with the tercentenary year. Holland and England opened the ball in 1920, the Dutch concentrating on the religious principles of the Pilgrims. A stained-glass window showing the embarkation was placed in the English Reformed Church at Amsterdam : Leyden had an exhibition of documents referring to the Pilgrims as it had done in 1888, and there were more celebrations at Delftshaven. The mayor of

Southampton and the deputy mayor of Plymouth, England, joined these celebrations; the burgomaster of Leyden in return visited Plymouth for the pageant staged for ten days around 6 September. It was held in a drill hall at Millbay on the site of a prisoner of war barracks which, ironically, had held American prisoners in the war of 1812.

Only the year before, Plymouth had returned the Virginian-born Lady Astor as the first woman member of the British Parliament, and she brought down many English and American notables for the key celebrations at the Mayflower Stone on Monday 6 September, to which all 400 performers in the pageant marched in their costume. On the Sunday before there were American preachers in the principal churches with two descendants of Elder Brewster among them, the Bishop of Connecticut (the Rt Rev C. B. Brewster) at St Andrew's and the Bishop of Newark, New Jersey (the Rt Rev E. S. Lines) at Charles.

Across the Atlantic the tercentenary was principally marked by a reshaping of Plymouth's waterfront. The wharves were removed, two stretches of newly-made land pushed out into the sea on either side of the Rock, and its position adjusted so that it rested on the beach again, where high tides could wash around it. An iron gate kept vandals away on the seaward side while letting the tides sweep in, and a vast classical canopy by Messers McKim Mead & White and given by the Colonial Dames of America was built over it. Up on Coles Hill a sarcophagus was built to receive the Pilgrim bones which had been in the old canopy and, close by, a bronze statue representing Massasoit was set up by the Improved Order of Redmen. The symbolism of the Indian chief on this particular site is a little strained, but his attire is considered to be authentic and enables the visitor to see what sort of neighbours the Pilgrims had. Up on Burial Hill two genuine cannons, a minion and a saker of the kind that the Pilgrims mounted for their first defence, were set up as a gift from England.

The climax came with pageants and processions; finally on 29 November 1921 the presidential yacht escorted by four battleships and six destroyers steamed in. The deputy Mayor of old Plymouth, Isaac Foot, himself a Methodist and a historian as well as the father of four distinguished politician sons, was there with representatives of Holland and of all the American historical and patriotic societies.

President Warren Harding made the major speech, though the large crowd kept its biggest welcome for the vice-President, Calvin Coolidge, a favourite son of Massachusetts. The speeches and the pageant are largely forgotten but the focal point of the Pilgrim legend took the shape it still has, and after the vicissitudes of 150 years the Rock was not only in one piece but in a position where the legend was credible.

MORE MEMORIALS

Over the next fifty years, as the motor car made people more mobile, so the number of visitors steadily increased. The oldest houses in Plymouth, Mass, several dating back to the seventeenth century, were restored and refurnished and made more attractive for visitors to see. The Brewster Gardens were laid out along the Town Brook and a statue of the Pilgrim Maiden set up by the spring, to demonstrate that there were not just the Pilgrim Fathers. The Society of Mayflower Descendants acquired the old Winslow House and made it the headquarters of their order. On a pilgrimage to Europe in 1928 they left more plaques in their wake, notably in Leyden. In 1955 there were 152 such pilgrims, who flew the Atlantic and left even more plaques behind. The monument at Southampton acquired one, as did the churches at Babworth and Scrooby. One was also presented to Dartmouth, which caused a little embarrassment because until that time the Devon port had no Mayflower memorial at all. So one was hastily prepared in Bayard's Cove, though it was not unveiled until two years after this particular visit.

The sequence of tablets is not a true guide to the points visited on this pilgrimage, for old Plymouth declared that one monument to the true Pilgrims was enough. It had improved on the original by moving the stone in the roadway of the pier close to the plaque in the wall and setting a small classical portico over it in 1934. It was paid for by a legacy from the 1921 Mayor, Sir Frederick Winnicott, but the city (an honour conferred on old Plymouth in 1928) had just torn down an eighteenth-century watch house which, with its granite pillars, always served as a photographic background to the Mayflower Stone. The little temple in some ways compensated for the lost background.

In America too the memorials were growing. In 1930 the Massachusetts Bay Colony Tercentenary Commission set up markers like English inn signs on historical sites, so that places linked with the Pilgrims, like Merry Mount in Quincy or the wading place at Middleborough which the travellers to Massasoit used to ford a river, can be identified by the passing motorist. In Holland as well the signs had grown, with one of the most useful marking the point of departure from Delftshaven. Leyden set up a Pilgrim room in the municipal museum, De Lakenhal. In England Edward Winslow was remembered by tablets in the cathedral at Worcester, where he was educated, and at St Peter's Church, Droitwich, where his father was churchwarden. Miles Standish has his tablet in Chorley Church, Lancashire, as well as his statue on Captain's Hill, Duxbury, Mass.

Nor was Christopher Jones of the *Mayflower* forgotten. His parish church at Rotherhithe was rebuilt in 1715 and at the 250th anniversary of this event the American ambassador in London unveiled a tablet to Jones in the church, rather pleasantly set under the memorial to a sea captain buried there in 1625. Carved on it is a bas-relief of a ship which could have been drawn from *Mayflower II*. The churchyard where Christopher Jones was buried is a children's playground now with swings and slides; gaunt tenements and mills fill the lanes that Pepys walked, but there is still romance in driving down Cathay Street and Jamaica Road and Paradise Street, past East India Wharf and the Bombay Warehouse to find it. Rotherhithe has had a Mayflower Street running down to the river since 1936 (it was called Prince's Street before); and when the church honoured Jones, the public house across the road, the Spread Eagle and Crown, whose back looks out on the gravel beaches of the river where *Mayflower* berthed so often, changed its name to Mayflower. In the same way of course the Duke of Brunswick Inn facing the waterfront at old Plymouth became the Mayflower when the tablet appeared in the pier opposite, and the Saracen's Head on the turnpike at Scrooby became the Pilgrim Fathers about 1920.

Only lonely little Sturton-le-Steeple, lost on the banks of the Trent, seems without any marker. Its inn has not changed its name; it is still the Reindeer. Only five Americans in five years signed their name in the church visitors' book. In spite of the power stations just north and south of the village, whose forests of steam-belching cooling towers dominate the flat plains where once Sturton's many-pinnacled church tower was the only eminence, and the V-bombers of the Royal Air Force which wheel over all these Pilgrim villages, Sturton seems unchanged by time. Perhaps John Robinson would have preferred it so.

PLIMOTH PLANTATION

The two major developments in Plymouth, Mass, since the Second World War are Plimoth Plantation and *Mayflower II*. Plimoth Plantation, an educational, non-profit-making corporation, was founded by Henry Hornblower II, a Boston stockbroker who had spent all his boyhood holidays and weekends in Plymouth, studied anthropology and archaeology at Harvard, and read history under Admiral Samuel Eliot Morison, an authority on the Pilgrims and early New England. In 1945 Mr Hornblower launched the idea of building a Pilgrim memorial village. A replica of the First House near the Rock attracted 339,000 people in its first year. A 1627 house was added, and then a replica of the Fort Meeting House.

William Baker had been set to work by the Plantation to prepare plans for a full-scale *Mayflower II* when a group in England offered to build such a ship, sail her across the Atlantic and present her to the Plantation. Warwick Charlton was the mainspring of the English group, and with many problems and financial headaches the ship was eventually built and sailed across in 1957. That was also the year in which Jamestown was celebrating the 350th anniversary of its foundation; the fact that *Mayflower II*'s voyage and her welcome in Plymouth by vice-President Nixon, with all the attendant pageants and publicity, stole the headlines was an accident but it did not endear the Plantation to the Virginians.

Mayflower II was found a permanent berth beside State Pier, close to Plymouth Rock. The First House and the 1627 House remain nearby but another site at Eel River, two miles to the south, was found which physically reproduced the site of the Pilgrim settlement. The Fort Meeting House was moved there, and Plymouth as it was in 1627 recreated, as closely as scholarship and research could make it to the original. The accent throughout has been on historical truth. 'This is no Disney-land', to quote a member of the staff. Sheep and hens wander about the village and their droppings are real; maize is grown as the Pilgrims grew it and meals are cooked in the houses on wood fires. The furnishings are those which early wills show to have been in the houses, the visitors can see precisely what life in Plymouth 1627 was all about, and the correctly-costumed hosts in each house talk about different aspects of the early life.

Plimoth Plantation is now beyond doubt the major centre of Pilgrim research. It has commissioned and published special studies, carried out excavations, created a library and an unmatched source of material for the discerning visitor. In its first twenty years it has had almost 4,700,000 visitors, including 200,000 students in school groups. The annual budget is over $600,000 (£250,000). The staff of thirty-five fulltime, and over a hundred seasonal persons, includes scholars and researchers. But apart from its contribution to historical knowledge, its essential importance is that the ordinary people can see and hear and smell the life of their ancestors. Some of the child visitors have never before seen chickens with legs and feathers, had no idea of what they looked like outside the deep freeze, never seen sheep with lambs at their feet; it emphasizes the value of all this in an increasingly urban society.

The most recent development in Plymouth itself is a wax museum at the back of Coles Hill, where behind a pillared Colonial front a series of tableaux traces the Pilgrim story from Boston Jail to the courtship of John Alden and Priscilla Mullins. The exhibition has the essentials of the story and all the romantic additions; waves rock the boat which approaches Plymouth Rock and storm-music and lightning add to the effect. Children lap it all up; 'it's real cool Mom' said a small boy. Not everyone is happy, but it does serve the kind of tripper who can hardly be bothered to climb out of a car to look at the Rock.

Plimoth Plantation has been a valuable force in the modern

Plymouth, setting high standards in accuracy, presentation, and even in the souvenirs and books it makes available. The past President of the Pilgrim Society, Ellis Brewster, is a trustee of the Plantation and his son, William S. Brewster, a governor. Close links are kept with all the older establishments in Plymouth, and with the descendants of the first families whose pride and joy is in the old houses. Through the Chamber of Commerce, which maintains a visitor information centre in the town, a collective ticket is available which takes the visitor into Pilgrim Hall, all the old houses, *Mayflower II*, and the Plantation. But it must be accepted that today the fount of knowledge about the Pilgrims is not with the true descendants and inherited lore of the old families, but with the skilled researchers of the Plantation.

PLYMOUTH TODAY

Modern Plymouth is very dependent on the summer resident and the tourist, yet has managed to avoid the excesses of the holiday trade. Opposite the *Mayflower II*'s berth are the gift shops and the hot dog stand and the restaurant; but they are not obtrusive and, by American standards, even restrained. There are more restaurants on the Town Wharf, where the working lobstermen and the seven or eight draggers (trawlers) still have their base, but even here there are twice as many charter fishing boats for sport.

In 1830 the population of 5,000 was kept busy by a hundred coastal trading vessels and fishing boats, five iron mills, two cotton mills, and three ropeworks. The Pilgrims noted the 'excellent strong kind of flax and hemp' the first day they went ashore at Plymouth, and Plymouth Cordage Company, with Ellis Brewster at its head, was in business until the late 1960s, the last of the old manufactories of any size in the town. The 1965 population of 15,000 showed an eleven per cent increase over the previous ten years, with the wholesale and retail trades employing nearly fifty per cent of the working population. Both the growth of the population and the over-reliance on shops for employment shows the holiday trade to be booming; indeed the population is nearly trebled in the summer months. But the closure of the last two woollen mills and the reversion of the cordage factory to general warehousing in the late 1960s administered a shock to a town which for over a century had had an industrial basis. It had not been well-paid industry, however, and had brought in a large number of Portuguese and Italian workers.

Facing yet another crisis in its long story, Plymouth raised $125,000 (£52,500), partly from private sources, partly from Federal and State funds, to lay out the 200 acre industrial park. Two or three industries had committed themselves by 1969 to moving there, and there were negotiations for more. Outside the industrial park, two other new industries had come into the town, the harbour was being dredged and a new sea wall built to improve yachting facilities, and an oceanographic growth linked to an existing development. A $100,000,000 plus (over £42,000,000) nuclear power station at Rocky Ledge, two and a half miles south of the town centre, will be operational in 1971.

Since the vast farming grounds of the Middle West developed, the hinterland of Plymouth has gone back to forest. The Old Colony towns have the trees close round their perimeters, and some of the hamlets are now no more than a few houses in a clearing in the woods. Some have gone altogether, and only the little graveyard encircled by trees shows that a village once existed. It is a general New England pattern, even more marked in Maine. Forty miles to the north Boston flourishes, an urban area of over 3,000,000 people whose prosperity was founded by its fine harbour. This New England metropolis is linked by good roads to Plymouth which is also served by a well-appointed airport.

Local government has not changed. The elected Board of Selectmen meets weekly for routine business under the chairman; major decisions go to a town meeting but instead of everybody participating there are 213 representatives who meet at least once a year. Six elementary schools, a campus-style high school, and twenty churches serve the community. The Chamber of Commerce is active and forward-looking.

It is a far cry from the simple agricultural community of the 1620s, fishing and trading with the Indians with wampum beads, to airports and nuclear power stations. From it all Plymouth has emerged a normal, simple, New England town, spread out along the shores of a cheerful harbour. One can imagine that the founding fathers of Scrooby and Leyden would find it pleasant, with friendly people and clean attractive houses. They would like to have heard the remark of a non-native resident now active in Plymouth : 'It's a good town to bring up children in.'

CHAPTER NINE

The Place in Men's Minds

AMERICANS HAVE SHOWN a particular aptitude for the revival and restoration of their old houses, villages and towns. They can staff them with people in period costume as if it were the most natural thing in the world. At Plimoth Plantation a teenage girl who would normally be in a mini-skirt sits on a hillside as she tends the sheep and instinctively wraps her cloak round her bent-up legs to keep out the cold; without knowing it she is a living illustration of how her grandmother ten times removed behaved. One can see this in many places. Old Sturbridge village in Massachusetts recreates a New England country town of a century and a half ago; Strawberry Banke at Portsmouth, New Hampshire, is a new venture near the trading-post site of the Pilgrims' first neighbour, David Thompson, using the original houses to recreate the eighteenth century; Mystic in Connecticut brings back the great sailing days of the nineteenth century. Of all these the most famous, and the most extensive, is Williamsburg.

There the old capital of Virginia, which the State government abandoned for Richmond in 1780 to escape the British ships in the War of Independence, has been under restoration since 1927. John D. Rockefeller jr and his family have put $80,000,000 (over £34,000,000) into the project, and nearly all the houses were there waiting for restoration. It exudes the pride of Virginia in its history and is the major attraction of this Colonial Historical National Park. Probably most visitors go from Williamsburg to Yorktown where they can savour the full patriotic fervour of the place where Lord Cornwallis surrendered a British army in 1781, and the United States clinched its independence. Many do go the other way down the parkway to Jamestown, the first English settlement in North America, but it has these strong rivals close at hand.

Part of the original site of Jamestown has been washed away

by the River James. Before World War II the visitor could only be shown a commemorative obelisk, a ruined church, and a few foundations. Now there is a reproduction of the first settlement, and an interpretation centre where paintings, models, costumed figures, documents and artefacts explain the original colony. There are also full-scale reproductions not of one seventeenth-century ship but three, the *Susan Constant*, the *Godspeed*, and the *Discovery*, to show its visitors. Yet a Jamestown man has wryly observed, 'I shall clobber the next visitor who asks me "which is the *Mayflower?*" ' When Robert Kennedy of Massachusetts was introduced to an assembly of Virginian lawyers his host said,

> Everybody knows that the *Mayflower* in 1620 arrived before the Jamestown ships in 1607. Virginia is a country of the Lees and the Randolphs. They came one at a time. Boston is the country of the Adamses and the Kennedys and they happened all at once.

The *Mayflower* cult, the Pilgrim legend, was built up in New England at the end of the eighteenth century and developed in the first half of the nineteenth. It was spreading west into the prairies by the mid-century. The new population, the main waves of immigrants from Europe, entered the United States by the Yankee ports and either stayed there or moved west, assimilating and taking with them, in addition to their own cultures, the ideas and legends of their new land. The ideas of New England were carried across the continent. Philadelphia and Baltimore were the most southern ports to receive any real number of immigrants, but even from these two ports the new families tended to move south and west behind the Appalachian Mountains. So the old South with all its colour and gallantry and atmosphere of the old gentry remained isolated. In any case such ideas were anathema to the newcomers; most of them had fled from Europe to escape feudalism and the oppressions of the gentry, the landed families.

The American Civil War underscored this. From 1861 to 1865 the South was fighting for the continuation of slavery, and for the maintenance of privilege. The South had hardly changed since the War of Independence. For thirty years before 1861 there had been a campaign against slavery, and inevitably it carried with it an attack on the ideals and beliefs of the slave-owning states. After the war there was no burst of generous reconciliation. The southern states were treated like conquered territory. The northern Republicans were determined to break the power of the old gentry, the natural white leaders of the South, to prevent the southern Democrats regaining political power. There was not a Democratic President again until Grover Cleveland in 1884, and he only won the election because of the character of his opponent. Thus there was half a century in which the South suffered, and its way of life endured constant condemnation.

The Jamestown settlers had shown courage and determination. They had established themselves when others, north and south, had failed. They too had faced hunger, decimation by disease, hardships in the forests, attacks from the Indians; had gone through all sorts of adventures before they won through. But originally the settlers were all men, paid by employers to establish their colony. When they began to get their roots down a shipload or two of women were sent over and married the settlers. It was an Anglican, High Church, Tory establishment, and even though this background produced George Washington and Peyton Randolph, who might have been the first president had he lived, it was the newcomer Patrick Henry from the backwoods who stirred the Tidewater planters in 1765 to vote against the Stamp Act.

Virginia in fact had been founded at Jamestown as an extension of England. It was a late flowering of Elizabethan England, the age of Drake and Shakespeare when the old country found both her strength as a seapower and her voice, when the Englishman asserted himself and found he could contain and overcome the enmity of Catholic Europe, when he found the New World stretched before him and old Spain and Portugal unable to keep their grip upon it. Richard Grenville and his fellow men of Devon received the queen's first licence to 'join to the Christian faith and also to our dominion and amity' the colonies he proposed. This had been one of the inspirations of Francis Drake's voyage round the world and prompted him to 'take possession' of California for the queen in 1579. There was nobility and high purpose in the early colonising attempts, choice spirits like Ralegh and Gilbert and Grenville were engaged upon it. But by 1607 the old queen was dead and the first fires of English inspiration with her. The morose King James was on the throne, and the merchants of London were the motivating powers behind the finally successful colony of Jamestown. Only Ralegh of the high adventurers was alive to see it happen, and he was already under suspended sentence of death, a prisoner in the Tower. One must give all honour to the men of Jamestown who endured much and proved that such an enterprise was possible. Without their example the worried English community in Leyden would never have thought their venture possible.

THE WRITERS AND BOSTON

If Jamestown lacked the religious fervour and the desperate necessity of Plymouth, it also lacked the writers. Captain James Smith served Jamestown well and to his propaganda we owe all our early knowledge of Jamestown, the stories of Pocohontas and the like. But Smith told so many extravagant tales in his life, from the furtherest side of Muscovy to the interior of Virginia, that they are taken with a pinch of salt. Probably this is unfair; more and more his stories become credible as more knowledge unfolds. Reading *Purchas His Pilgrimes* where Smith's accounts are followed by Winslow's stories of the early Pilgrim days it is clear that Winslow observes more closely and has a more vivid pen. Smith was a soldier, Winslow a scholar. The Pilgrims had not only Winslow but Bradford as well; the latter's narration may owe much to Winslow, but Bradford was a man of profound thought who could not only reach down to the motives that inspired the Pilgrims but could set them down so that over the centuries they come fresh and clear. John Smith left Virginia in 1614; from then on he was the arch-propagandist for New England, and Virginia lost its chronicler. Plymouth has been better served by its writers and propagandists than ever Jamestown was.

Bradford's book came to light when literary America was dominated by the New England renaissance, when Boston and its bookseller at the corner of School Street and Washington Street was the centre of American thought. Henry Ward Beecher, Ralph Waldo Emerson, Nathaniel Hawthorn, Oliver Wendell Holmes,

Henry Wadsworth Longfellow, Amy Lowell and her brother James Russell Lowell, Harriet Beecher Stowe, Henry David Thoreau away in the woods, John Greenleaf Whittier: it is hardly possible to think of them without the sonorous Christian names. Their faded books displayed at the Old Corner Bookstore in Boston, where most of them were published, bring back memories of the book-cases of one's youth. They have been closed books, save to students, for most of this century. Last century these authors dominated the thought of the young and forward-looking in the country, and in their ranks were the leading abolitionists and opponents of slavery.

Longfellow could trace his ancestry, through his mother, back to the Pilgrims, and in his *Courtship of Miles Standish* he added another story to America's favourite legends. Emerson, the 'sage of Concord', married a Plymouth woman in the drawing-room of the Winslow house there, and her memorial is by the Pilgrim Spring down by Town Brook. Mrs Stowe's first book was *The Mayflower*, though she is remembered for *Uncle Tom's Cabin*. It was not that these writers were directly trumpeting the Pilgrim story or the Pilgrim morals. There were basically men and women of New England, mainly of nonconformist background, and, though they reached out from their Puritan backgrounds to explore new ideas, the strength and virtues of that background never left them. They did not push the Pilgrim legend so much as create the mental atmosphere in which it could become acceptable. In the same way the *North American Review* and the *Atlantic Monthly*, the most influential American journals of the day, came from the same publisher and the same writers. The propaganda direct came from Mrs Sarah Josepha Hale, editing first the Boston *Ladies' Magazine* and then the *Godey's Lady's Book* of Philadelphia; it was she who eventually persuaded the United States to make Thanksgiving Day a national holiday.

Boston was still keeping pace with New York as a mercantile and banking centre for the rapid western expansion of the states. Through its railways it reached out into the prairies; through its financial strength it was in touch with the business men and the developers, the men of power right through the country; its politicians were still strong in the nation's affairs. As in England, many of the great merchants were liberal, nonconformist, sober men. The qualities extolled in their churches of honesty, uprightness, probity, fair dealing with one's fellow men, were the qualities that brought their own reward in business. The stern unbending merchant, thrifty and careful, was the staunch church-goer. That these qualities brought their reward on earth was part of divine justice; provided one prayed on Sundays and cared for the weak, gave a share of this world's riches to succour the deserving poor, then one's reward would also come in heaven. These were qualities with which the Pilgrims were invested. Their *aqua vitae* and the way they missed their beer were forgotten as temperance became respectable, their strict family life was held up for admiration, and the steel engravings and narrative pictures of the Pilgrims show the drab and colourless clothing that was more true of the nineteenth century than of the seventeenth. The Pilgrims could be easily bent, and were, to represent all that was best in New England uprightness.

One may well ask why Boston turned back to the Pilgrims and not to its own founders, why they went to Brewster and Bradford rather than Winthrop and Dudley. The answer is in Boston still:

> And this is good old Boston,
> The home of the bean and the cod,
> Where the Lowells talk to the Cabots,
> And the Cabots talk only to God.

But neither the Cabots nor the Lowells were there in the early days. The proper families whose houses still look down on the tree-lined, gas-lit avenues of Beacon Hill, where the chestnut leaves fall quietly on the redbrick pavements of Joy Street and Mount Vernon Street and Louisburg Square, date back to the merchants and ship-owners of the nineteenth century. They were new men, with no roots going back to the first fathers. To evoke the founders would be to expose their newness; far better to extol the Pilgrims who were common ancestors for everybody, whose descendants were numerous and widespread but not particularly important outside sleepy Plymouth and Duxbury, busy building its little ships that offered no rivalry to the great fleets of Boston. There was too a faint odour of over-righteousness and intolerance and autocratic rule about the early Massachusetts Bay settlers; the tolerant and (within limits) democratic Pilgrims were free from any such taint.

THE COMMON ANCESTOR

This was an idea that all America was to find acceptable, that here were common ancestors not only of the rich men of Boston but of the poor, newly-arrived immigrant as well. The Pilgrims may not have made it from log cabin to White House but they were poor men who had made good, men who had come with nothing but their courage and their bare hands and made themselves a home. They had fled the tyrannies and oppressions and the grinding poverty of Europe where the have-nots seemed destined for all time to remain so; they had braved the perils of the ocean and the privations of a stinking ship; they had arrived in a world of strange manners and men and all kind of problems, and made a good life for themselves. For many of the later European newcomers the English language was as unfamiliar as the words of the Indians to the Pilgrims. These immigrants faced perils in the eastern cities of America that were just as real and as threatening as anything the Pilgrims had known. Those who pressed out to the frontiers found that they had to carve their fields from the forests, build their homes, hold off the Indians. They could understand deep in their hearts the true meaning of Thanksgiving at the end of the year. For New York and the eastern cities it might just mean fireworks and a feast, but even in those crowded streets there were many new families from Europe who could count their blessings on Thanksgiving Day.

Parallel with this came the enormous success of the General Society of Mayflower Descendants; one might detect in this another natural human desire. The old South had gone down in the Civil War and its white leaders were ostracised, while the rich North waxed and grew fat. But the old South had the ancestry; the families there could reach back with pride to colonial days, to genuine gentry. The ancestry of the North was as good but smacked a little of the newly-rich, the *parvenu*. The desire of the man who has made his pile to have a coat of arms comes out. But the North had the Pilgrims, and they were the best ancestors of all. The Mayflower Society was, perhaps unconsciously, an answer to the Colonial Dames and the Daughters of the American Revolution. To have a *Mayflower* name was almost as if the neighbours touched their caps; to have a guaranteed *Mayflower* ancestor was nearly as good and probably three times as many Americans as the 24,000 who have joined the society make this claim. Even Boston put up a tablet in Spring Lane to proclaim that 'Mary Chilton lived here'. In every state the Chapters of the Mayflower Descendants start their annual dinners with the five kernels of parched corn, as did Daniel Webster and his hosts in Plymouth Court House in 1820, to commemorate the hungry days of their ancestors, before moving on to the rich foods of the affluent society.

In this century the Colonial Dames, the Daughters of the American Revolution and the Mayflower Descendants have been used as figures of fun, have been sneered at by those with no claims of entry. As the nineteenth-century morality became unacceptable so the Pilgrims suffered from having been turned into nineteenth-century figures. In defence their apologists have stressed their humanity, their humour, claimed the bright clothes and denied the starched white collars that the old pictures insisted on, declared that there was a difference between them and the Puritans. It became almost an offence to suggest that the Pilgrims had been Puritans, when of course they had advanced beyond Puritanism, the desire to purify the church from within, by leaving it. The word 'puritan' by this time had lost its theological meaning and become a way of life; almost a dirty word. Just as Lytton Strachey in England held up the great Victorian figures to ridicule, so did the new American historians deny the premises of their predecessors, that the Pilgrims had brought with them all that was good in American life.

The historians were answered by Samuel Eliot Morison, a member of a proper Boston family, a descendant of Priscilla Mullins, and a professor of history at Harvard and California and Oxford, with seven battle honours and admiral's rank in World War II, of which he is the official naval historian. In a speech to the Mayflower Descendants of New Hampshire in 1936, reprinted, revised and much quoted since, he declared:

The place of the Pilgrim Fathers in American history can best be stated by a paradox. Of slight importance in their own time, they are of great and increasing significance in our time, through the influence of their story on American folklore and tradition. And the key to that story, the vital factor in this little group, is the faith in God that exalted them and their small enterprise to something of lasting value and enduring interest.

He accepted that only three American institutions had been started by them; registry of deeds, civil marriage, and the Congregational church. But, he went on :

The story of their patience and fortitude, and the workings of the unseen force which bears up heroic souls in the doing of mighty errands, as often as it is read or told, quickens the spiritual forces in American life, strengthens faith in God, and confidence in human nature.

He exalts the stout-hearted idealism of Bradford's History which all Americans respect, even when they cannot share it.

Thomas Carlyle had said something like this nearly a century before when he wrote about the sailing of the *Mayflower*. 'It was properly the beginning of America. There were struggling settlers in America before . . . but the soul of it was this.' But even Americans who have never read Carlyle know the Pilgrim story and embroider its legends. A man who lives on Merry Mount in Quincy came out in the rain to speak to a visitor photographing the tablet commemorating Thomas Morton, 'a merry Englishman', as his scandalous goings-on are euphemistically recorded. He said he had had a series of Negro maids in his house at one time, all brought up from the deep South, and all turned out to be pregnant. 'It's the ghost of Tom Morton', declared his doctor neighbour, 'he thinks they're Indian girls.'

The Pilgrims also qualify for the American establishment, for they were white, Anglo-Saxon, and Protestant, complete 'Wasps' to use the acid term. A writer in *Time* defined the Wasps as 'at the narrowest a select band of wellheeled, well-descended members of the eastern establishment; at the wildest they include Okies and

Snopeses, "Holy Rollers" and hillbillies.' They still make up about fifty-five per cent of the United States population and however mixed the American stock has become, however strong the 'ethnic blocs' courted by politicians, they are still the backbone of America and still a real power.

In the American schools today the younger children hear the Pilgrim story in a modified nineteenth-century form. The spiritual values, the heroism, the excitement is all given to them, but they escape the faintly hysterical moral overtones of Mrs Hemans that their grandparents, and even some of their parents, endured. By the time they reach high school and scepticism sets in, the youngsters are cynical about the Pilgrim story, as they are of so many accepted values. But the rebels, the drop-outs, and the young intellectuals, are beginning to find that the new honest teaching about the Pilgrims has the ring of truth in it. The Pilgrims too were rebels, drop-outs, people who refused to accept the standards of the day and were willing to risk everything, their homes, their families, their comforts, because they would not conform. Norman Mailer, increasingly the voice of the young rebel, who constantly preaches that America is a sick country, takes it even further :

> We are sick, we're very sick, maybe we always were sick, maybe the Puritans carried the virus and were so odious the British were right to drive them out, maybe we're a nation of culls and weeds and half-crazy from the start.

Maybe? Not even Norman Mailer in his Cape Cod cottage can escape the Pilgrim consciousness.

Many read Mailer: few go all the way with him for, like all prophets, he paints the extreme picture. The unthinking rebels reject everything; for their parents to have accepted something is enough to condemn it in their younger eyes. But the rebels who examine what they are rebelling against, who are protesting against the materialistic society and all its false values, find that this is just what the Pilgrims were doing. In time youth finds that its new discoveries, like sex, are not really original. There were Harvard students who, during the early days of the 1969 troubles on the campus, realised that there had been a rebellion in America before them; they were to be found on the Freedom Trail through

Boston, learning something of what their forefathers had fought about. Stripped of the false values that the centuries have laid upon the Pilgrims, cleansed of all the images that have been wished upon them by men who tried to find in them a justification of their own way of life, the men and women of the *Mayflower* have much to say to the young rebels of today. What is more, the Pilgrims were constructive rebels. They were not content with denouncing one form of society, they persevered until they had built another which did give life and reality to their ideals.

THE EUROPEAN MEMORY

It is not remarkable that the Pilgrims should have been forgotten in England and Holland, and that memories there should only have been stirred after the American interest had awoken. As Morison says, they were unimportant in their own time. Scrooby and the little villages of the north Midlands of England have no learned societies nor large scholarly communities to remember the village sons. The odd antiquarian parson has produced a booklet of his church and remembered the part his predecessors' parishioners have played in history, but the visiting Americans are chiefly responsible for what knowledge there is. A vague local pride now exists in having had some part in founding the United States. At Scrooby a new housing estate bears the Mayflower name and the oldest house in the village (a long way from the manor house) has a worn tablet saying 'William Brewster lived here. Post to Queen Elizabeth and King James I, 1594-1607.'

In Holland the mass of the people have heard of the Pilgrims, and are aware that they stayed for a time in their country, but it reaches them in the schools as a point of interest linked with their English lessons, rather than as a matter of history. Even in Leyden, where from time to time there are organised parties of Dutch school children, English tourists, visitors from the States and members of the American forces in Europe visiting the site, the memory seems lightly held. Each year a Thanksgiving Day service is held in the Pieterskerk at Leyden, and at the English Church in Amsterdam, but the congregation is mainly American. John Robinson's house in Leyden made way for an almshouse built in 1683 from funds left by two French religious refugees, Jean Pesijn and his wife Marie de la Noy. It is remembered now as the Jean Pesijnhofje, but almost as much because the wife's family, de la Noy, were ancestors of Franklin Delano Roosevelt, as for the Pilgrim's sojourn. What does move the Dutch mind is that they had to fight long and bitterly against the Spanish to establish the right to worship as they wished, to be Protestant and not Catholic, and in the Pilgrims they see fellow sufferers for the cause.

In both countries there is also the kind of pride in being linked with the *Mayflower*, with the foundation of the United States, that there is in the individual who went to school with the man who is now top of the tree. As the United States has risen to dominate the western world so this pride has increased. As American culture has flowed back into Europe, and particularly through the common language into England, so the legends and tribal lore of the Americans have spread into these countries. Englishmen may often know little more about the *Mayflower* than they do about George Washington and the cherry tree, but at least they have a part in the *Mayflower* story. In the Channel ports the information bureaus have had to know the historic links to direct the Americans; in Southampton and Dartmouth and Plymouth the *Mayflower* is now part of each town's history and the English pay their homage as well. There is also the commercial angle which the tourist trade has not been slow to seize upon, and on both sides of the Atlantic the words 'Mayflower' and 'Pilgrim' are used for all kinds of commercial enterprises. Here again the old joke about the common language being the biggest barrier rings true; in the telephone directory of Boston, Mass, there are eighteen 'Mayflowers' and forty-five 'Pilgrims'. (The Pilgrim cinema shows restricted films to mark the march of time, offering such pleasures as *Take Me Naked*.) In the telephone directory of Plymouth, England, nine 'Mayflowers' appear and only two 'Pilgrims'. In America 'Pilgrim' is the emotive word, in England 'Mayflower'.

Southampton has a Mayflower Road (1911), a Mayflower Park (1955) opposite the memorial, and a Mayflower public house (1964). At the time when the memory of the Pilgrims was reviving in England, Southampton was too busy with its vast expansion as an outport of London, particularly in the passenger trade, to pay much attention to its history. Its great historic days in any case were earlier than the Tudor opening of the New World. On the West Gate the tablet puts the army of Henry V bound for Agincourt in 1415 above the Pilgrim Fathers' embarking in 1620. In the remains of its walls, in Bargate, in the Wool House where the cargoes for the carricks of Genoa were stored, in the archaeological museum in God's House—a corner tower of the walls—Southampton has tangible reminders of its great medieval days. These exercise its civic pride in history and even the Mayflower Memorial seems trapped between an ancient wall and a busy road to the docks, cut off from all but the determined sightseer.

Dartmouth came even later to consciousness of the *Mayflower*. From the late nineteenth century until the years after World War II it was in decline. The railway never came nearer than the other side of the river, and the steep landward approach make it still a difficult town for road transport. The few mail steamers which had used the port moved to Southampton in 1891. An important coal bunkering trade which began in 1878 was dead by 1939, killed by the advent of oil fuel, and the almost total disappearance of coastal trade. Trouble in the parish church, problems of land ownership in the cramped town, all kept it too busy to fret about a chance ship in 1620. Only the creation of the Britannia Royal Naval College for training the young officers of the navy, and after World War II the overflow of the tourist trade from nearby Torquay, kept Dartmouth solvent and enabled it in post-war years to claim its rightful place in the Pilgrim story.

MOTHER PLYMOUTH

Of all the English ports of call Plymouth had its memory stirred earliest, and at a time when it was receptive and prospering sufficiently to afford such a luxury. If one feels that Drake and the *Golden Hind* in which he sailed round the world, and the Hawkins family who built up the town's Elizabethan prosperity, should be its true heroes, then Plymouth has the wrong balance in its visible memorials. The telephone directory lists nine 'Mayflowers' and two 'Pilgrims' against seven 'Drakes' and two 'Golden Hinds'; Mayflower Street flourishes while Drake Circus is disappearing in the city's reconstruction. There is not a single enterprise using the name Hawkins, no street name, not even a tablet anywhere. (In Victorian Plymouth, when the tablets and the memorials were sprouting, there was some guilt felt about the Hawkins family because they had been the first Englishmen to enter the slave trade.) Drake has his statue on the Hoe but in the ancient harbour where the great voyages are recorded Drake has not a single mention.

So Plymouth has promoted the Pilgrims to the level of its greatest sons, and pays them more honour than any other town in England or Europe. The name attracts Americans of course because it is the name of the Pilgrim town. The boasting claim on the banners of the Rotary Club of Plymouth, Mass, 'America's home town', is not without meaning. Plymouth, England, is a long way from London and its poor air communications upset Americans to whom taking a plane is normal and catching a train almost as peculiar as waiting for a stage coach. Yet it does attract American industry; Acheson Colloids of Port Huron, Michigan, established its main European factory there in 1911. Since World War II the city has welcomed twenty-six new factories in its endeavours to diversify its employment, and ten of them are American controlled. They range from Brown & Sharpe of Rhode Island, through household names like Wrigleys to Texas Instruments. They are attracted by the industrial skills which overflow from Plymouth's basic business of naval shipbuilding, the under-employed female population, and the clean air, but there is also an intangible feeling of homeliness which even the most hard-headed efficiency expert feels about moving to Plymouth, even the one in England. In fact the city almost does better with American industries and resident American executives than it does with American tourists. They come, but it is a problem to persuade any but the most intrepid to leave the fixed American-in-England route of Buckingham Palace, Oxford and Stratford-on-Avon.

Apart from the factories, which mean nothing to the man in the street, and even if there was never another American tourist, the *Mayflower* story would remain part of the consciousness of Plymouth people, part of the city's history. For fifty years Plymouth was the port from which England set out to win control of the Atlantic; in the first great flowering of English expansion, in the golden age of action and poetry Plymouth was the stepping-off place for all the great deeds of derring-do. It was home port to the great admirals and sea-captains, it was the point at which words and ideas changed into action. Plymouth men were among those leaders, Plymouth above all supplied the crews, the followers, the men who died across all the oceans of the world to make England into not just a nation, but for three centuries the dominant nation of the world. For those three centuries England had to fight to maintain that role, and Plymouth as a naval base was always in the front line of that fighting.

The ordinary man is ignorant of the details but he knows all this in his bones. In his lifetime or in that of his parents, Plymouth has been nearly destroyed because she was once again in the front line of a fight for decency and civilisation. It is part of a continuing story. He knows that in those early days, when the Atlantic was the new battleground of Plymouth men, there were long and desperate attempts to plant a new colony on the far shores. The best leaders of Plymouth, some of its most adventurous sons, tried and failed. Then a group of ordinary people who did not even have enough sense to set out in the spring, but poked out into the Atlantic at the worst time of the year, sailed out of Sutton Pool and succeeded. Plymouth is not very sure where they came from, or who they were, but knows they did it; the city not only recognises their valour, but knows more than most places how much they achieved.

Plymouth people knew why they went, at the time. That was why their kindness was honoured by the Pilgrims keeping their town's name for the new settlement, which they might so easily have rechristened. Plymouth was then a firmly Protestant town, and tough enough to have purified its parish church in the way it wanted; when stopped by a king it demanded another church, and got it, and cheerfully stood a three-year siege in which the death-rate soared to three times the normal figure, because of its religious beliefs. By the time the Congregational leaders came back in 1891 there had been a large influx of Irish from Cork and the other southern counties of Ireland, so many that Plymouth became the centre of a Roman Catholic diocese with a Roman Catholic cathedral. But in Victorian times St Andrew's, the mother church, was so 'low' that its vicar almost degenerated into a mob leader when the 'high' church of St Peter was founded to begin what Plymouth regarded as Popish practices. To read the attacks which decent churchpeople and nonconformists made upon brother Christians is shame-making now, but it shows the fierceness with which Plymouth held its stern Protestant beliefs. Until the early days of this century the vicar of the town's second church, Charles, would end Matins and Evensong and remove his surplice before mounting the pulpit to preach the sermon in everyday clothes, like the lecturers of the original Pilgrim times.

Now Charles is a ruin; St Andrew's still 'low' and St Peter's still 'high', but they talk to each other and to the Catholics and the Baptists and the Congregationalists. It is a much more tolerant world, but the fires that sent Brewster and Bradford and their companions across the Atlantic have not so long died down, and Plymouth has not forgotten the heat of those fires. Today this strife between sects seems ridiculous. Our great doubt is whether God exists at all; the only Pilgrim doubt was about the best way to serve him. Once they had resolved this in their minds they were able to achieve what mere men of action, Christians, devout Christians perhaps but not desperate Christians, could not do.

'WHERE'S THE ROCK?'

Plymouth, Mass, is on the road to Cape Cod. As the French flock to the Pointe de Raz in Finisterre and the English to the Land's End, so do American tourists to the Cape. The Kennedy compound is an added attraction now, and in the southern arm of the Cape the antique shops cluster thicker than commuters in rush hour. It is not the most eastern point of America; Maine can claim that, but the Cape is the most dramatic. 'A man may stand there and put all America behind him', wrote Thoreau. All through the summer the cars hurl along US Route 6, and at the end the Pilgrim Memorial reminds them that this is not the end but the beginning of America. For those that come down from Boston, Plymouth is right beside the highway. For those who come from New York and the rest of the United States, the road from Providence through Taunton and Plymouth is little longer than that through Fall River and New Bedford. So apart from its inherent tourist attraction Plymouth is on the road somewhere, and a million people a year are estimated to look down at the Rock in its bearpit; 250,000 a year go aboard *Mayflower II*.

There is a steady stream into the visitor information centre. The serious visitors put down their $3.50 (£1 9s od) for five historic houses, Pilgrim Hall, Plimoth Plantation, and *Mayflower II*—the group ticket saves $2 (16s 8d). The mass of callers has one of two opening questions: 'Where's the Rock?' or 'Where's the boat?'. Just 'the boat'; to specify would be superfluous. Watching the flow from beside the Rock is instructive. The eyes of the small children always light up. The teenager with his girl flicks his cigarette ash over the rail (the sand is brushed clean regularly) before they rush over the road and up the steps of Coles Hill. Too many adults can hardly heave themselves out of the car and away from the radio for a cursory look.

It is after all just an old bit of stone with a date carved in it. A disappointment perhaps after thundering up Interstate 95, or down the Southeast Expressway. But still it draws its millions of people for there it all began, the big adventure that is the United States of America, there the common ancestors of all of them first came ashore. They do not mouth, with Mrs Hemans, 'yea call it hallowed ground' or even remember Bradford's lines:

As one candle may light a thousand, so the light here kindled has shown to many, nay in some sort to our whole nation.

But they come. The place has a meaning though they cannot give it words and would not want to. Here ordinary men and women like themselves, with their children, came ashore in the snow and the frost of a New England December, after crossing the ocean in a boat hardly big enough to take a present-day car. Here ordinary men and women succeeded against impossible odds. They had so little, and achieved so much. Nice people, kindly, friendly, homely, from whom grew the greatest nation in the world.

The one thing which carried them through was their faith, their belief that God was with them and watched over them and suc-coured them. They had the faith that twentieth-century man has lost, and so desperately needs, and rarely finds in his rushing up and down. In them was the simple virtue, the content with small things that has gone out of life. These were the people of the first frontier, and now the last is crumbling. They knew they were Pilgrims; we are not sure what we are. When the last words are said, when all the scholars and the clever people have analysed and philosophised, the one simple fact remains. They believed in God, and that made all things possible. We can watch men land on the moon, we can see hearts transplanted. We believe in General Motors and Standard Oil and ICI and computers, but we can stand in Plimoth Plantation and smell the woodsmoke, and the simple verities come back. It is because these men and women had in them the basic, eternal virtues, the simple faith that is lost to our generation, that they are remembered, and honoured, across the world.

Appendix

List of Passengers in the *Mayflower*

This list is taken from William Bradford's History. (Those from whom descent can be proved are marked with an asterisk; those who died in the first winter are marked with a dagger.)

The names of those which came over first, in ye year 1620. and were by the blessing of God the first beginers and (in a sort) the foundation of all the Plantations and Colonies in New-England; and their families.

MR JOHN CARVER†; KATHRINE†, his wife; DESIRE MINTER; & 2. man-servants, JOHN HOWLAND*, ROGER WILDER†; WILLIAM LATHAM, a boy; & a maid servant, & a child yt was put to him, called JASPER MORE†.   8

MR WILLIAM BREWSTER*, MARY*, his wife; with 2. sons, whose names were LOVE* & WRASLING; and a boy was put to him called RICHARD MORE*†; and another of his brothers. The rest of his children were left behind, & came over afterwards   6

Mr EDWARD WINSLOW*; ELIZABETH†, his wife; & 2. men servants, caled GEORG SOWLE* and ELIAS STORY†; also a little girl was put to him, caled ELLEN†, the sister of RICHARD MORE.   5

WILLIAM BRADFORD*, and DOROTHY†, his wife; having but one child, a sone, left behind, who came afterward.   2

Mr ISAAK ALLERTON*, and MARY*†, his wife; with 3. children, BARTHOLOMEW, REMEMBER*, & MARY*; and a servant boy, JOHN HOOKE†   6

Mr SAMUEL FULLER*, and a servant, caled WILLIAM BUTTEN. His wife was behind, & a child, which came afterwards   2

JOHN CRAKSTON†, and his sone, JOHN CRAKSTON.　　　2

CAPTIN MYLES STANDISH*, and ROSE†, his wife.　　　2

Mr CHRISTOPHER MARTIN†, and his wife†, and 2. servants, SALAMON PROWER† and JOHN LANGEMORE†.　　　4

Mr WILLIAM MULLINES*†, and his wife*†, and 2. children, JOSEPH† & PRISCILLA*; and a servant, ROBART CARTER†.　　　5

Mr WILLIAM WHITE*†, and SUSANA*, his wife, and one sone called RESOLVED*, and one borne a ship-bord, caled PEREGRIENE*; & 2. servants, named WILLIAM HOLBECK† & EDWARD THOMSON†.　　　6

Mr STEVEN HOPKINS*, and ELIZABETH*, his wife, and 2. children, caled GILES*, and CONSTANTA*, a doughter, both by a former wife; and 2. more by this wife, caled DAMARIS & OCEANUS; the last was borne at sea; and 2. servants, called EDWARD DOTY* and EDWARD LITSTER.　　　8

Mr RICHARD WARREN*; but his wife and children were lefte behind, and came afterwards.　　　1

JOHN BILLINTON*, and ELEN*, his wife; and 2. sones, JOHN & FRANCIS*　　　4

EDWARD TILLIE†, and ANN†, his wife; and 2. children that were their cossens, HENERY SAMSON* and HUMILLITY COPER　　　4

JOHN TILLIE*†, and his wife*†; and EELIZABETH*, their doughter.　　　3

FRANCIS COOKE*, and his sone JOHN*. But his wife & other children came afterwards.　　　2

THOMAS ROGERS*†, and JOSEPH*, his sone. His other children came afterwards.　　　2

THOMAS TINKER†, and his wife†, and a sone†.　　　3

JOHN RIGDALE†, and ALICE†, his wife.　　　2

JAMES CHILTON*†, and his wife*†, and MARY*, their dougter. They had an other daughter, yᵗ was maried, came afterward.　　　3

EDWARD FULLER*†, and his wife*†, and SAMUELL*, their
sonne.   3

JOHN TURNER†, and 2. sones†. He had a doughter came
some years after to Salem, wher she is now living.   3

FRANCIS EATON*, and SARAH*†, his wife, and SAMUELL*,
their sone, a yong child.   3

MOYSES FLETCHER†, JOHN GOODMAN†, THOMAS WIL-
LIAMS†, DIGERIE PREIST†, EDMOND MARGESON†, PETER
BROWNE*, RICHARD BRITTERIGE†, RICHARD CLARKE†,
RICHARD GARDENAR, GILBART WINSLOW.   10

JOHN ALDEN* was hired for a cooper, at South-Hampton,
wher the ship victuled; and being a hopfull yong man, was
much desired, but left to his owne liking to go or stay when
he came here; but he stayed, and maryed here.   1

JOHN ALLERTON† and THOMAS ENLISH† were both hired,
the later to goe m^r of a shalop here, and ye other was reputed
as one of ye company, but was to go back (being a seaman)
for the help of others behind. But they both dyed here, before
the shipe returned.   2

There were allso other 2. seamen hired to stay a year here in
the country, WILLIAM TREVORE, and one ELY. But when
their time was out, they both returned.   2

These, bening aboute a hundred sowls, came over in this first
ship; and began this worke, which God of his goodness hath
hithertoo blesed; let his holy name have ye praise.

———

Note: *Mayflower* left Plymouth with 102 passengers aboard.
William Butten, servant to Samuel Fuller, died on the voyage but
during the passage Elizabeth Hopkins gave birth to a son, Oceanus,
so that 102 people still arrived at Cape Cod. There Susanna White
bore a son, Peregrine but Dorothy Bradford was drowned and
three other people died, so that ninety-nine reached Plymouth. In
his totals for each paragraph Bradford made the Tinker family
two when it should be three, which may explain the 101 figure
often quoted.

Bibliography

THE BASIC BOOK is William Bradford's history, *Of Plymouth Plantation*, and a most satisfactory edition that of Wright & Potter, 1898, containing 'A report of the proceedings incident to the return of the manuscript to Massachusetts.' For the early years *Mourt's Relation*, published in 1622 and probably mainly the work of Edward Winslow, is just as important. The two do not always agree on dates or order of events; I have tended to accept *Mourt's Relation* as being written nearer the event. A pleasant edition with a scholarly introduction and pictures of Plimoth Plantation is *A Journal of the Pilgrims at Plymouth*, with introduction by Dwight B. Heath (Cornish Books, New York, 1963).

For Captain John Smith and other contemporary accounts of the New World, *Purchas His Pilgrimes* is vital. Volume 19 of the set published by MacLehose of Glasgow and Macmillan of New York in 1906 contains most of the material. *Chronicles of the Pilgrim Fathers* in the Everyman Library, edited by John Masefield, contains Winslow's *Goode Newes from New England* (1624) and Nathaniel Morton's *New England's Memoriall* (1669). *The Pilgrim Story* (Memorial Press, Plymouth, Mass) is a compilation by William Franklin Atwood of Bradford and Winslow, in paperback form.

For the English background, as well as the religious aspects, there is Dr John Brown, *Pilgrim Fathers of New England* (Religious Tract Society, London, 1906) and Walter Burgess, *John Robinson Pastor of the Pilgrim Fathers* (Williams & Norgate, 1920). The state of the church in Plymouth is clarified by Henry Nicholson, *Records of the Church at George Street, Plymouth* (Doidge, Plymouth, 1870); Rev John Ingle Dredge, 'A Few Sheaves of Devon Bibliography' (*Transactions* Devonshire Association, 1889 and 1890); Rev S. G. Harris, 'Samuel Heiron' (*Trans* DA 1892). For Plymouth generally there are the invaluable R. N. Worth *History of Plymouth* (Brendon 1890) and his *Calendar of the Plymouth Municipal Records*, (1893); and for Dartmouth the admirable Percy Russell, *Dartmouth* (Batsford, 1950).

For *Mayflower* and *Mayflower II* : Dr J. W. Horrocks, 'The Mayflower' (*Mariner's Mirror*, 1922); Dr R. C. Anderson 'A Mayflower Model' (*Mariner's Mirror*, 1926); William A. Baker, *The New Mayflower, her design and construction* (Barre Gazette, Mass, 1958), 'Deck Heights in the Seventeenth Century' (*American Neptune*, 1962), and 'Notes on a Shallop' (*American Neptune*, 1957); Alan Villiers, *Give Me a Ship to Sail* (Hodder & Stoughton, 1958); and Dr Rendell Harris, *Finding of the Mayflower* (Longmans Green, 1920).

American histories are numerous : I have used George W. Southgate, *The United States* (Dent 1942); Frank Thistlewaite, *The Great Experiment* (Cambridge University 1961); and for the pioneer days Marion Starkey, *Land Where our Fathers Died* (Constable 1961), R. N. Worth, 'The Plymouth Company' (*Trans DA* 1882), Henry F. Howe, *Early Explorers of Plymouth Harbour* (Plimoth Plantation & Pilgrim Society, 1953), and Dr A. L. Rowse, *Expansion of Elizabethan England* (Macmillan 1955).

Early nineteenth-century Plymouth, Mass, is recorded in William S. Russell, *Guide to Plymouth and Recollections of the Pilgrims* (1846) and the memorials are well recorded in Allan Forbes, *Towns of New England and Old England* (Tudor Publishing Co, 1936). Special aspects of the early settlers are thoroughly examined in two Plimoth Plantation publications, *Three Visitors to Early Plymouth* (ed. Sydney V. James, 1963) and Ruth A. McIntyre, *Debts Hopeful and Desperate: Financing the Plymouth Colony* (1963). There are a number of valuable pamphlets published by the General Society of Mayflower Descendants; the Old South Association of Old South Meeting House, Boston; the Pilgrim Society, notably Rose T. Briggs, *Plymouth Rock, History and Significance* (1968) with wise comment and interesting old photographs; and Plimoth Plantation, notably Samuel Eliot Morison's important 1936 New Hampshire speech, *The Pilgrim Fathers, their Significance in History* (1951). The handbooks of the old houses in

Bibliography

Plymouth, published by Plymouth Antiquarian Society, Pilgrim John Howland Society and Sparrow House Inc are useful.

For general reading on the subject the most popular works are Morison's *Story of the Old Colony of New Plymouth* (Alfred A. Knopf, New York, 1956) and George F. Willison *Saints and Strangers* (Heinemann, London, 1966).

Acknowledgments

THIS BOOK could not have been written without much help from old friends, and from friends made in the course of the journeys undertaken while writing the book. In Plymouth the Town Clerk, Stuart Lloyd Jones, the City Librarian, William Best Harris, and the Local History Librarian, Marion Beckford have, as always, answered every call. The Vicar of Yelverton, Prebendary T. R. Owen, guided my theological reading. In the National Maritime Museum, Greenwich, the Director, Basil Greenhill, and the Keeper, George Naish, guided me on the nautical problems. In Rotherhithe the basic research was made by George Bickford, Michael Borne and his wife Patricia; in Chalfont St Giles, Ann Way worked on the Mayflower Barn at Jordans. In Holland a vast amount of research and photography was done by David and Ati Borne, who were my eyes.

Across the Atlantic my way was smoothed with much kindness and hospitality from Gladys and Charles Helmholtz, who from Portland, Maine, to Providence, Rhode Island, were the souls of kindness; they must have my deepest thanks. In Boston I had much help in the Massachusetts State Archives from Dr Richard Hale and Mr and Mrs Leo Flaherty, and in the Old State House Mrs Ropes Cabot of the Bostonian Society guided my footsteps. William Baker gave me much time and help over *Mayflower II*, and with his wife Ruth entertained me royally. In Plymouth, Mass, I was well looked after by Philip Seiler and Marie at the Hobhole House; Allan Stapleton, Managing Director of the Chamber of Commerce, primed me on the modern problems, and his assistants, Pat Fama and Gladys, were delightful guides to the Cape. Forrest Wentworth of the General Society of Mayflower Descendants was a courteous guide and mentor in the Winslow House.

Plimoth Plantation could not have been more generous with pictures and books, time and knowledge. There I have to thank the Director, David Freeman; the Public Relations Director, Lawrence

Acknowledgments

Couter, who took me under his wing; and the Curator, Cyril Leek Marshall and his wife for their hospitality and conversation. It was heart-warming to find everywhere in Plymouth that the words 'I'm from Plymouth, England' opened all doors; ministers, rotarians, the hostesses of the old houses, everybody made me feel I had a second home town.

At the end of the road Mr Couter and the Plantation Research Department very nobly read the typescript; I am grateful to them for many wise comments. All the way along, my wife, who first persuaded me that I could write the book, supported me loyally, drove me many hundreds of miles, and took many of the photographs. Finally, with our younger daughter Sarah, she spent many days compiling the index.

Index

Index

Index

Index